MW00679708

Chemical Dependency: Theoretical Approaches and Strategies Working with Individuals and Families

ABOUT THE EDITOR

Dana G. Finnegan, PhD, CAC, is Co-Director and Co-Founder of Discovery Counseling Center in Milburn, New Jersey, a center specializing in counseling services for individuals affected by alcoholism and sexual identity problems. She is a faculty member of the Advanced School of Alcohol and Drug Studies, Rutgers University Center of Alcohol Studies, Continuing Education Seminars, Rutgers University Summer School of Alcohol Studies, and the New Jersey School of Alcohol and Drug Studies where she has presented courses on the dynamics of supervision in alcoholism treatment agencies, practical group techniques and approaches for counseling alcoholics, teaching clients how to change, and sexual identity issues in recovery.

Dr. Finnegan, currently a board member of the National Association of Lesbian and Gay Alcoholism Professionals (NALGAP), was Co-Founder and Co-National Coordinator of that organization. She is also Co-Chair of PRIDE National Advisory Board.

She has written, with Emily McNally, *Dual Identities: Counseling Chemically Dependent Gay Men and Lesbians,* (Hazelden, 1987), and with T. McGinnis, *Open Family and Marriage: A Guide to Personal Growth* (C.V. Mosby, 1976), as well as several papers and articles on helping homosexual alcoholics. She has presented workshops and training seminars on counselors as change agents, group and individual counseling techniques, and counseling gay/lesbian alcoholics to regional and national conferences and organizations. She is an editorial board member of *Alcoholism Treatment Quarterly,* and is the new Senior Editor of the *Journal of Chemical Dependency Treatment.*

Chemical Dependency: Theoretical Approaches and Strategies Working with Individuals and Families

Eileen B. Isaacson
Guest Editor

Journal of Chemical Dependency Treatment
Volume 4, Number 1

The Haworth Press
New York

Journal of Chemical Dependency Treatment, Volume 4, Number 1 1991.
JOURNAL OF CHEMICAL DEPENDENCY TREATMENT is published biannually at The Haworth Press, Inc., 10 Alice Street, Binghamton, NY 13904-1580.

The *Journal of Chemical Dependency Treatment* addresses the specific needs of chemical dependency counselors, social workers, psychologists, nurses, physicians, clergy, educators and other professionals who provide direct clinical services to drug dependent clients and their families. Each thematic issue takes an in-depth look at a treatment problem and provides practical "how-to" approaches to addressing that concern with clients. While the journal emphasizes clinical technique and method, theory and research are integrated to support clinical experience. Each issue is guest-edited by a recognized specialist in the field who selects authors with substantial clinical experience to present their views and approaches. Our goal is to provide a forum for the exchange of ideas, concepts, methods and issues of import to the field of chemical dependency treatment. We want to build a body of knowledge that supports and enhances quality care for the chemically dependent person and his or her family.

ABSTRACTING & INDEXING: Articles in *Journal of Chemical Dependency Treatment* are selectively abstracted and/or indexed in: *Alconarc Database; Criminal Justice Abstracts, Family Resources Database; Index to Periodical Articles Related to Law; Mental Health Abstracts, Psychological Abstracts; (and PyschINFO); Referantivnyi Zhurnal (Abstracts Journal of the Institute of Scientific Information of the USSR);* and *Special Educational Needs Abstracts.*

MANUSCRIPTS: Those interested should request "Instructions for Authors" from the Editor, Dana Finnegan, PhD, 708 Greenwich Street, Apt. 6D, New York, NY 10014.

BUSINESS OFFICES: Except for overseas sales representatives, all subscriptions and advertising inquiries should be directed to The Haworth Press, Inc., 10 Alice Street, Binghamton, NY 13904-1580. Telephone (607) 722-5857.

SUBSCRIPTION INFORMATION: Subscriptions are on a per volume academic year basis. The following prices are *for the current volume only* for the USA, Canada, and Mexico:

US$: 28.00 individuals (paid by personal check);
US$: 45.00 institutions (e.g., social service agencies, clinics, hospital departments, and paid by institutional check);
US$: 105.00 libraries and subscription agencies (e.g., whenever purchased for libraries either directly or through subscription agencies).

Subscriptions must be prepaid. Postage & handling is included in the price. Payment in USA or Canadian funds only; if paying by Canadian check, please add in the additional amount to cover the current exchange rate. All *back volumes* are available at the current rate plus 25% surcharge.

FOREIGN ORDERS (Outside USA, Canada and Mexico): 40% above USA rate. All foreign subscriptions are mailed via AIRMAIL.

SUBSCRIPTIONS THROUGH AGENCIES: Subscriptions through any subscription agency subject to publisher's credit check of subscription agency and payment record history of subscription agency. Renewals through agents must be prepaid 60 days prior to renewal cycle of journal, which is: November 1st for calendar-year journals and July 1st for academic-year journals. Library subscribers will be notified if subscription agent does not remit renewal payments on this schedule.

CHANGE OF ADDRESS: Please notify the Subscription Department, The Haworth Press, Inc., 10 Alice Street, Binghamton, NY 13904-1580 of address changes. Please allow six weeks for processing; include old and new addresses as well as both zip codes.

SPECIAL NOTES REGARDING:

(a) LIBRARY PHOTOCOPYING OF JOURNAL ARTICLES
(b) PERSONAL PHOTOCOPYING & REPRODUCTION OF ARTICLES

(a) LIBRARIES may freely photocopy journal articles for traditional multiple library use, including multiple copies for reserve room use, extra copies for faculty/student dissemination, interlibrary loan, and network use. Haworth has no "per-charge" fee and does not participate in any individual article royalty system;

(b) INDIVIDUAL USERS may also reproduce articles for classroom teaching purposes; our only restriction is the reprinting or anthologizing for re-sale.

Dedicated with Love
to
Charles, Sharlene and Bernard

ABOUT THE GUEST EDITOR

Eileen Isaacson, EdD, ACSW, CAC, is Director of the Brunswik Counseling Group and Training Institute. Dr. Isaacson's experience includes twenty years of work in the chemical addiction field. She is a New Jersey licensed Marriage Counselor, Certified Alcoholism Counselor, and Certified Addiction Specialist. She is an adjunct faculty member of the Rutgers University Graduate School of Social Work and on the faculty of the Rutgers University Advanced School of Drug and Alcohol Studies and the New Jersey Summer School of Alcohol and Drug Studies. Dr. Isaacson has designed and delivered a variety of training programs in individual, family, and group counseling focusing on chemical dependency. As consultant to UMDNJ-CMHC at Piscataway, New Jersey, she developed The Institute for Chemical Dependency, a model program integrating knowledge and case application, and providing a clinical practicum for mental health, alcohol and drug professionals. Dr. Isaacson received the New Jersey NASW Trailblazer Award in 1989 for service in the addiction field.

Chemical Dependency: Theoretical Approaches and Strategies Working with Individuals and Families

Journal of Chemical Dependency Treatment
Volume 4, Number 1

CONTENTS

Preface

From my perspective as a physician and psychiatrist, traditionally trained in medicine and psychiatry and with about twenty years of experience in the field of addiction medicine, as well as my more recent experience (about ten years) with systems—orientated, recovery—orientated and self help treatment programs and chemical dependency, I was struck by the interdisciplinary nature of this work.

Dr. Eileen Isaacson has edited and produced, in my opinion, a valuable contribution to the fields of chemical dependency, individual psychotherapy, and family therapy. This volume is a comprehensive and interdisciplinary synthesis of these fields, drawing on a variety of approaches, sources of information, and disciplines (even medicine and psychiatry) in achieving this synthesis. This synthesis, in turn, provides an excellent and basic foundation for counsellors, therapists, and—even—physicians who work in this often bewildering field for the incorporation of family therapy models and techniques, individual therapy models, and recovery-oriented approaches into their treatment, applicable to a wide variety of types of patients and patient populations. The several papers in this volume fit together well as a basic textbook in family therapy, individual therapy, and the addictions. It can be read by beginners in the several fields (family therapy, individual therapy, and chemical dependency), for example, for a grounding in the three basic "schools" of family therapy (i.e., the structural model; the strategic model; and Bowen's approach). It can also be read, consulted, and even used for reference by the more experienced practitioner, for example, for concepts, approaches, and practical guidance in working with addicted women, blacks, gay men and lesbians, and Latino males. Since Dr. Isaacson reviews and summarizes the papers and content of this volume in her "Introduction," I will not reiterate that summary in this *Preface*. Suffice it to say, however, that the volume is carefully crafted: It starts with material providing an overview of family therapy, especially as applied to the chemically dependent; then provides information about the special populations noted above; and it concludes with an interdisciplinary discussion about the mentally ill chemical abuser.

My impression from having read many "Prefaces" over the years is that one of the purposes of a preface — aside from the obvious one of "setting the stage" for the volume to follow — is to present supportive and complimentary comments about the volume: to "say nice things" about it. In this case, this is not difficult to do: Dr. Isaacson's volume is timely, informative, well put together, interdisciplinary, well written (especially with the liberal use of case studies throughout almost all of the individual papers), and provides an important contribution, in my opinion, to the fields of family therapy, individual therapy, and chemical dependency. As a physician in a field sometimes oriented against "physicianly" (i.e., biomedical) approaches, I will find this volume extremely useful to me in my own work. Dr. Isaacson herself, I note, has been working in these fields in a variety of capacities for a number of years. By sharing her views, experience, and knowledge — as well as those of her colleagues — through *Chemcial Dependency: Theoretical Approaches and Strategies Working with Individuals and Families*, she has made a valuable contribution to the professional community.

Daniel P. Greenfield, MD, MPH, MS
Managing Partner
Brown & Greenfield Physician Consultants (Millburn, NJ)

Department of Psychiatry
Albert Einstein College of Medicine/
Montefiore Medical Center (Bronx, NY)

Introduction

The field of chemical addiction has evolved over the past several decades, initially working with the individual from a variety of perspectives including physiological, psychological and sociological. Recognition of the importance of working with the families of addicted individuals developed gradually out of the family therapy movement of the '50's and '60's, taking hold as an intervention tool in the '70's.

This writing underscores the importance of working with both the individual and family as part of a comprehensive biopsychosocial approach in assessment, intervention and treatment of chemical addiction. It is intended to provide a framework for assessment and intervention with individuals and their families. Theory and practice are integrated focusing on: Family Systems and Chemical Addiction; Individual and Family System Dynamics of Chemical Addiction; Application of Psychodynamic and Family Systems Theories to Chemical Addiction; Special Intervention Strategies (Neuro-linguistic Programming, Planned Family Intervention with Johnson Institute Method, Family Therapy and Twelve Step Programs); and Intervention with Special Populations Characterized by Chemical Addiction (Women, Gays/Lesbians, Hispanic Males, Blacks, and the Mentally Ill Chemical Abuser).

An historic overview of family systems and chemical addiction is presented in the first article, "Chemical Addiction: Individuals and Family Systems," to provide a foundation for working with the individual as part of the family system. Basic to addressing chemical addiction as it relates to the individual/family interaction is an understanding of the development of addiction in the individual as a function of early psychological development and the family factors which influence and maintain the homeostasis of dependency. This article is presented as a framework for the subsequent articles.

Donna Richardson describes the use of family systems therapy in the article "Structural and Strategic Family Therapy Techniques: Application to Chemically Dependent Families." Ms. Richardson discusses specific components of the models in working with the case of an alcohol and drug addicted female who has been sexually abused, a problem often surfaced in working with chemically dependent clients. In a second case of a male alcoholic, the use of contracting is discussed as part of a process intermediary to obtaining treatment. A step-by-step process illustrates the therapist's role in engaging the individual and family, demonstrates the dynamics of the family, and discusses intervention strategies in the progress of treatment. Ms. Richardson is a therapist in private practice and clinician at the Family Relations Center of the University of Medicine and Dentistry of New Jersey, Community Mental Health Center at Piscataway.

The use of a model integrating work with the individual and family is presented and discussed in "Psychodynamics and Family Systems: A Model for Chemical Addiction Counseling." The reader is referred to the first article on "Chemical Addiction: Individuals and Family Systems" which provides a framework for individual and family dynamics as they relate to addiction. The importance of ongoing assessment and intervention with each of the models is suggested as a way of dealing with the underlying dynamics of individuals while working toward systemic change in the family. Application of psychodynamic and family systems components to the case of an alcohol/drug addicted male is presented.

Ellen Faber and Beverly Keating-O'Connor present a model for family intervention in "Planned Family Intervention: Johnson Institute Method." Components of the model are described and a discussion of myths, family rules and dynamics of addiction are discussed in relation to the use of planned family intervention. Ms. Faber and Ms. Keating-O'Connor provide an overall understanding and use of the intervention for therapists. Ms. Faber's *Handbook for Intervention* is also recommended to therapists interested in this area. Ms. Faber is Director of Intervention Associates, an intervention program to motivate individuals and families to treatment; her experience consists of twenty years of working in alcoholism treatment. Ms. Keating-O'Connor has been involved in the addiction field for eleven years and has clinical experience working at the

University of Medicine and Dentistry of New Jersey and the Medical Center at Princeton, New Jersey.

Chelly Sterman demonstrates the use of Neuro-Linguistic Programming (NLP) as a psychotherapeutic tool in working with addicted individuals and their families in "Neuro-Linguistic Programming as Psychotherapeutic Treatment in Working with Alcohol and Other Drug Addicted Families." Techniques such as "reframing" to address "traumatic childhood experiences" are related to addiction using case examples. Practitioners interested in further reading in this area will be interested in her recent publication *Neurolinguistic Programming in Alcoholism Treatment*. Ms. Sterman is in private practice in New Jersey and has worked in a variety of inpatient and outpatient chemical abuser treatment settings. She is a Master Practitioner in Neurolinguistic Programming.

Emily Schroeder discusses the importance of integrating twelve-step programs and family therapy in "Family Therapy and Twelve-Step Programs: A Complementary Process." Family therapy and twelve-step programs are described specifically as they relate to the treatment and recovery processes. Clear descriptions and examples are offered to clinicians in addressing the complex integration of these vital approaches in dealing with chemical dependency. The use of family systems and step programs during stages of active dependency, early sobriety, and later sobriety is presented. Ms. Schroeder is Executive Director of Family Systems Network, a private practice in New Jersey. Her experience includes extensive work in alcoholism rehabilitation programs.

Carolann Kane-Cavaiola and Diane Rullo-Cooney discuss issues related to chemically addicted women and their families in "Addicted Women: Their Families' Effect on Treatment Outcome." The problems faced by women in terms of social stigma, childcare problems and economic status are presented as blocks to women obtaining necessary treatment. Ms. Kane-Cavaiola and Ms. Rullo-Cooney stress the importance of treating the families of chemically addicted women in case discussions and provide recommendations for improving treatment. The practitioner in the field may be interested in reading Ms. Kane-Cavaiola's writings: "Basics of Adolescent Development for the Chemical Dependency Professional" and "Continuing Care for the Chemically Dependent Adolescent." Ms. Kane-Cavaiola is Director of the Center for Drug and Alcohol Prevention and Treatment at John F. Kennedy Medical Center in Edison, New Jersey. Ms. Rullo-Cooney is Clinical Supervisor at John F. Kennedy Medical Center.

Michael Shernoff and Dana Finnegan describe how counselors can work with chemically dependent gay men and lesbians in "Family Treatment with Chemically Dependent Gay Men and Lesbians." Issues of societal, family and individual homophobia are discussed as they relate to treatment. The importance of identifying conflicts related to sexual identity and early experiences of shame are explored in relationship to functioning and chemical use. Mr. Shernoff and Dr. Finnegan demonstrate family counseling interventions in their work with this population. Practitioners may be interested in Dr. Finnegan's writings including *Dual Identities: Counseling Chemically Dependent Gay Men and Lesbians*; "Alcoholism and Chemical Dependency"; and the "Lonely Journey: Lesbians and Gay Men Who Are Co-Dependent." Mr. Shernoff's writing, "Family Therapy for Lesbian and Gay Clients" is also recommended. Mr. Shernoff is founder and Co-Director of Chelsea Psychotherapy Associates in New York City, New York. Dr. Finnegan is Co-Director of Discovery Counseling Center in Millburn, New Jersey.

Myriam Laureano and Edward Poliandro discuss chemical dependency of male alcoholics and their families in "Understanding Cultural Values of Latino Male Alcoholics and Their Families: A Culture Sensitive Model." A framework for understanding the Latino culture and the impact of alcoholism on the family is presented. Ms. Laureano and Dr. Poliandro describe a Culture-Sensitive Assessment Model and apply the model to a case involving chemical addiction of a Latino male and his family. Ms. Laureano is in private practice in New York City, New York and is Co-Founder and Vice President of ABRAZOS, an organization for Latino professionals in the field of chemical dependence. Dr. Poliandro is in private practice specializing in psychotherapy of individuals and couples in recovery, and is a faculty member at Mt. Sinai School of Medicine.

Stacia Murphy discusses issues in working with chemically addicted Black clients and their families in "Treating Chemically Dependent Black Clients and Their Families." Ms. Murphy describes methods of addressing alcoholism, "the number one mental health problem in Black communities.'' The importance of a multi-modal approach to working with this population including eduction, social learning, cognitive restructuring and sociocultural aspects is presented. In discussing the importance of family involvement in treatment, the therapeutic relationship between the client and counselor regarding the importance of cultural sensitivity is underscored. Ms. Murphy is Executive Director, Alcoholism Council/Fellowship Center in New York City, New York.

Phyllis Reilly provides a comprehensive approach to working with the Mentally Ill Chemical Abuser (MICA) and family system in ''Assessment and Treatment of the Mentally Ill Chemical Abuser and the Family.'' Ms. Reilly describes guidelines for assessment and discusses critical issues such as pharmacological intervention as related to treatment. The use of family therapy as an intervention highlighting structural and strategic approaches is recommended, as well as family education and skill development programs as components in working with the client and family. Ms. Reilly has nineteen years of experience working in addiction including her current position as Director of Addiction Recovery Services at the University of Medicine and Dentistry, Community Mental Health Center at Piscataway. She is a founding director of the Association for the Mentally Ill Chemical Abuser (AMICA).

This publication is offered to practitioners working in the field of chemical dependency, mental health and other human service related fields with the intent of providing theoretical approaches and practical strategies in addressing individual and family addiction.

Sincere appreciation and gratitude is extended to Dr. Bruce Carruth, Dr. Irene W. Slone and Mr. Richard J. Russo for this encourgement. Special thanks goes to Shelley McLarnon for her support in completing this volume. Acknowledgement is extended to the contributing authors, colleagues who have supported on-going efforts in addressing chemical dependency and to the clients who serve as catalysts in promoting new learning.

Eileen B. Isaacson, EdD, ACSW, CAC

Chemical Addiction:
Individuals and Family Systems

Eileen B. Isaacson, EdD, ACSW, CAC

SUMMARY. This chapter provides a framework for understanding the dynamics of the individual and family systems characterized by chemical addiction.[1] Topics include: (1) Overview of Family Systems and Chemical Addiction Research; (2) Family Systems and Chemical Addiction; and (3) Dynamics of Individuals in Chemically Addicted Families. Models are presented for understanding the dynamics of addiction in the individual and the components of family systems which support the homeostasis of chemical dependency.

OVERVIEW OF FAMILY SYSTEMS
AND CHEMICAL ADDICTION RESEARCH

Overview of Family Systems

Family systems therapy as an outgrowth of the psychoanalytic movement developed in the 1950's through the pioneering work of Nathan Ackerman (considered the Father of Family Therapy) and Murray Bowen with schizophrenic patients. This marked a departure from an intrapsychic to an interpersonal focus into the 1960's. Other theorists and practitioners during this time included Gregory Bateson, Don Jackson, Jay Haley and Virginia Satir focusing on communications within the family system. As family systems grew, Bowen developed a conceptual framework working with the self in the system, as well as expanding the theory to include the extended

---

Eileen B. Isaacson is Director of the Brunswik Counseling Group & Training Institute in New Jersey. She is a New Jersey licensed Marriage and Family Therapist and Certified Alcoholism Counselor. Correspondence may be sent to the author at 7 Riley Rd., Morganville, NJ 07751.

family, and interactional patterns of triangulation within families characterized by dysfunctions including alcoholism. During the late 1960's and 1970's, family therapy was impacted by the structural movement which examined families from an hierarchical perspective; Salvador Minuchin (1974), Duncan Stanton and Thomas Todd (1982) are names associated with changing families by changing the organizational structure. The use of family systems as an intervention in chemical addiction came about in the 1970's and 1980's through recognition of the efforts of Minuchin and Fishman (1981), Stanton and Todd (1982), Fishman (1988) and Bowen (1978). Family systems in the 1980's and 1990's is witnessing the resurgence of the intra-psychic functioning of the individual and integrating individual dynamics with family therapy (Allen, 1988; Kaufman and Kaufman, 1979; Kirschner and Kirschner, 1986; Levin, 1987; Stierlin, 1987).

Recognizing the importance in addressing chemical dependency of the individual and the family system is the focus of this paper. At the same time, the value of family systems as a single intervention is limited. A growing awareness of the limitations of any one model in working with chemical dependency is underscored by increasing use of the Biopsychosocial Model (Chaudron and Wilkinson, 1988; Levin, 1990; Zucker and Gomberg, 1986) which incorporates biological theories (genetic and disease), psychological theories (psychodynamic, cognitive, behavioral, etc.) and sociological theories (socialization, sociocultural, systems). It is a basic assumption of this chapter that an understanding of biopsychosocial factors is essential in assessment, diagnosis, treatment and evaluation of addiction. Working with the individual and family system, therefore, necessitates the use of chemical dependency knowledge by the clinician as it relates to components of the biopsychosocial model in specific application to the family system.

Family Related Research
and Chemical Dependency

Research related to addiction and the family has focused on different factors in examining alcoholism versus drug addiction. This was in part due to: (1) a different profile for the drug addict compared to the alcoholic, i.e., the drug user was in his 20's while the alcoholic most often was a male in his 40's (this factor impacted all areas of an individual's life: stage of development, life cycle, etc.); (2) the social realities stigmatizing alcoholism and drug addiction; and (3) the political realities of resource allocation supporting separate treatment interventions for both groups.

The separate focus on alcoholism and drug addiction has resulted in identifying descriptive characteristics of the individual in the family; individual and spouse interactions with relation to the expression of communication; and behaviors supporting the addiction. This section presents some of the research findings specifically related to alcoholism and a summary of common characteristics related to alcoholism and drug addiction.

Studies related to alcoholism were characterized by an attempt to identify personality factors as potential predictors of alcoholism, behavioral and interactional patterns of the alcoholic and spouse, and impact of family alcoholism on children. While efforts to identify personality traits of the alcoholic were not successful, recent literature on the addictive personality identifies problems with object relations, grandiosity, poor self concept, and poor impulse control as characteristic of the alcohol and other drug addicted individuals (Miller, 1990). Communication problems such as blaming between spouses were noted by Paolino and McGrady (1977) and increased anger and difficulty in problem solving were cited by Jacob (1981) as related to increased alcohol intake. Medical problems, depression and problems in family cohesion were found in the spouses of those who relapsed. Hostility and aggressive interactions were also found to be characteristic of alcoholic couples (Billings et al., 1979). Problems in family cohesion, expressiveness and conflict were also found in families with alcoholism (Barry, 1990).

Research on children of alcoholics has found that they are often neglected and victims of physical or sexual abuse (Kaufman and Pattison, 1981). Studies relating drinking behavior of children and parents suggest: (1) children of alcoholics are at risk for alcoholism (Goodwin, 1971; Winokur, 1968); (2) that a positive relationship exists between "past and current parental drinking" and "alcohol/ drug addiction by children (Grichting and Barber, 1989). Harburg et al. (1990) identify a "fall off" effect evidenced by children (of parents who have high level consumption) who respond by moderating their own drinking. It is generally accepted that children of problem drinkers are more likely to become drinkers than children of non-problem drinkers (Kaufman, 1985; Pandina, 1990). Studies supporting the possibility of genetic transmission have included the adoption studies in Denmark (Goodwin, 1984) which suggested that sons of alcoholics were particularly vulnerable to alcoholism whether raised by alcoholic or non-alcoholic parents; and studies supporting identical twins more prone to alcoholism than fraternal twins (Kaij, 1960).

Similarities between alcoholism and drug addiction as they relate to the individual in the family have been noted by several writers. Kaufman (1985) stated "it is easier to describe the common aspects of drug abusers and alcoholics than tease out those that are unique," and summarized some of the common factors related to both addictions. They include: the use of alcohol or drugs as a symptom of family dysfunction; crises related to cohesion and fragmentation; a relationship between substance use and fusion between parents and children; multigenerational addiction; the male parent often distant or non-involved while the female parent is over-involved; the substance user often identified as the scapegoat of the family system; use of primitive defenses in dealing with conflict (e.g., denial projection and rationalization); high incidence of loss (death and separation); incidence of incest and family violence.

The outcome of research efforts over the past few decades has been instrumental in supporting the use of family work as an intervention in the addictions. Recent research suggests that involving the spouses of alcoholics positively influences drinking behavior of the alcoholic (McGrady, 1986). In addition involving family members in the treatment seems to influence reduction in drinking (Thomas, 1989). Literature dealing with drug addiction supports involving families in the treatment of individuals (Eells, 1986; Kaufman and Kaufmann, 1979; Lawson, 1983; O'Farrell, 1989).

While research findings are not conclusive in measuring the effectiveness of working with the total family, positive outcomes of intervention with subsystems of the family are increasing and the practical application of working with the individual in the family continues.

FAMILY SYSTEMS AND CHEMICAL ADDICTION

Family systems as an intervention in chemical addiction is rooted in systems theory. Functional family systems are characterized by a hierarchical structure of leadership, roles which support individual and family goal achievement, rules for communication and problem solving and intra family sub-group interaction as well as interaction with the environment, all of which are directed toward differentiation of family members. A systems model depicting the individual, family and environment is presented in Figure 1.

Family dynamics in chemical addiction exhibits dysfunctional behaviors and interactions which inhibit differentiation and support the continuation of chemical addiction. It is useful to have a basic understanding of theoretical assumptions and components of family systems relative to family addiction. Some underlying assumptions of family systems (Turner, 1986) and their expression in chemically addicted families (+) are summarized as follows:

1. The functioning of a family is greater than the sum of its parts, i.e., interactions by the subgroups of the family members. The family system promotes homeostasis (status quo) of the family by resisting change.

     + Interactions of members of the addicted family support the stability of the dysfunctional system characterized by the problem of addiction (Mapes, 1985; Steinglass, 1987).
2. Behavior of family members is interlocking.

     + In the addicted family individuals behave and interact in a way that maintains a rigid, closed system (limited interaction with a rigid, closed system (limited interaction with the outside environment). (Davis et al., 1974, Stanton and Todd, 1982).
3. Family problems are repeated over generations.

     + It has been noted by theorists that chemical addiction is commonly seen to repeat itself over two and three generations (Kaufman, 1985; Wegscheider, 1981; Winokur, 1968).

4. Individual symptoms reflect larger problems within the system.

+ Alcoholism is identified as a symptom which covers up other family problems (Stanton and Todd, 1982; Steinglass, 1987).

5. All families experience problems. Functional families are flexible in responding to problems while dysfunctional families are rigid.

+ Alcoholic families are characterized by rigid interactional patterns thereby limiting functional options (Bepko and Krestan, 1985; Wegscheider, 1981).

Dynamics of the addicted family can be further seen as a function of homeostasis and the supporting sub-components of codependency, including family roles, rules, and boundaries. Homeostasis and codependency are discussed in the following text (see Figure 3-IV, Family Codependency Patterns).

Homeostasis and Codependency

Homeostasis is defined as the family system functioning to maintain a status quo. It is generally accepted that alcohol or other drug use serves as the focus for family functioning which motivates individuals to behave in ways that maintain the use of the chemical and render the system resistant to change (Bowen, 1974; Brown, 1985; Kaufman, 1985). Maintaining components of the process include codependent interactions and behaviors of family members. Codependency is defined as reciprocal complementary interactions between individuals which maintain the relationships supporting continued addiction with specific reference to alcohol and drug use; the interactions have the effect of supporting behaviors related to continued use of alcohol or other drugs. Some of the codependent dynamics which may be component parts of the individual's past experience with chemical addiction interact to maintain the addictive behavior include fear, shame, guilt, anger, denial and rigidity (Potter-Efron, 1989). Family roles are behaviors adopted by individuals which support codependent interactions (Carruth and Mendenhall, 1989; Wegscheider, 1981) and in turn support the continuation of alcohol and drug use. Family roles including scapegoat, hero, mas-

FIGURE 1. Individual, Family and Environmental Systems

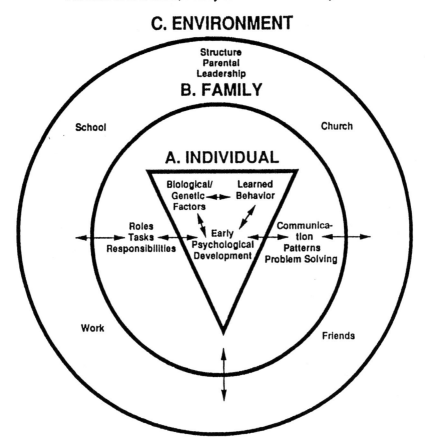

C. ENVIRONMENT

Structure
Parental
Leadership

B. FAMILY

School   Church

A. INDIVIDUAL

Biological/   Learned
Genetic ◄─► Behavior
Factors

Roles   Communica-
Tasks ◄──►   Early   ◄──► tion
Responsibilities Psychological   Patterns
Development   Problem Solving

Work

Friends

cot, enabler, have been identified by Wegscheider (1981). The roles assumed by an individual play out in the family rules of communication which have the effect of perpetuating the addiction by maintaining the paradox of the "family secret of addiction known to all." These rules encourage individuals to ignore the addiction by (a) avoiding intimacy (Don't trust), (b) not expressing affect (Don't feel), and (c) not discussing problems related to the addiction (Don't think or talk). Rules become part of the individual's behavior outside as well as inside the family system. In summary, rules and roles are part of the codependent interactions which support the homeostatic dynamics of addiction.

Boundaries in family systems separate the family from the environment, divide the family members into subsystems and differentiate individual members from each other. A healthy system has permeable boundaries wherein family members are part of the system and move easily in and out of the system. Boundaries of chemically addicted families have been identified as fragmented or enmeshed (Bowen, 1978; Minuchin and Fishman, 1981; Stanton and Todd, 1982). Enmeshed or fragmented systems are supported by roles and family rules which discourage individual growth. Systems with dysfunctional boundaries can be viewed as an interactive function of the lack of differentiation of individual family members.

DYNAMICS OF INDIVIDUALS
IN CHEMICALLY ADDICTED FAMILIES

This section discusses the following components which are essential to understanding chemical addiction of the individual and family: (1) Early psychological development of the individual (Figure 2); and, (2) Dynamics of the individual contributing to family codependency.

EARLY DEVELOPMENT: A POTENTIAL BASE
FOR ADDICTION

The development of individual addiction is the result of various influences which include biological/genetic factors, early psychosocial development, learned behaviors and family codependency patterns (interaction of roles, and rules) which are transmitted intra-family system and inter-family generational systems.

In an effort to understand the process of addiction, it is suggested that early psychological development of the individual provides the foundation for forming later relationships. The importance of early development is recognized as contributing to the sense of self and ego functioning in chemically addicted individuals (Bean et al., 1981; Bradshaw, 1988; Levin, 1987). A basic assumption of this writing is that early development is both a function of parent/family

FIGURE 2. Early Psychological Development

A) NORMAL DEVELOPMENT
1) Mahler
2) Freud
3) Erikson
B) POTENTIAL PROBLEMS IN CHEMICAL DEPENDENCY DYSFUNCTION

A) NORMAL DEVELOPMENT
1) EARLY PSYCHOLOGICAL DEVELOPMENT (Mahler, 1975)
SEPARATION/INDIVIDUATION

┌──── (Intrapsychic Separation /"Results in Sense of Identity") ────┐

Symbiosis/ Fusion with Mother	-Beginning Differentiation -Bond with Mother -Growing Awareness of Mother's Presence & Things Outside Self	-Practicing Self Identity -"I AM" -Body Differentiation -Autonomy from Mother	-Rapprochment -Development of Frustration Tolerance -Object Permanence	-Object Constancy -Maintains Representation of Love Object -Able to Integrate Good and Bad

AGE IN MONTHS (Approximate)

0   5   10/12   18   24   36

2) PSYCHOSEXUAL STAGES (Freud, 1966)

ORAL STAGE	ANAL STAGE	OEDIPAL STAGE
Dependency Needs/Trust	Separateness/Self Control	Sexual Identy

0   12   36   60

3) LIFE STAGES (Erikson, 1959)

TRUST VS. MISTRUST	AUTONOMY VS. DOUBT/SHAME	INITIATIVE VS. GUILT
Outcome: Hope	Outcome: Will	Outcome: Purpose

0   12   36   60

B) POTENTIAL PROBLEMS
IN CHEMICAL DEPENDENCY DYSFUNCTION

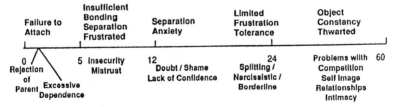

Failure to Attach	Insufficient Bonding Separation Frustrated	Separation Anxiety	Limited Frustration Tolerance	Object Constancy Thwarted

0   5 Insecurity   12   24   Problems with 60
Rejection   Mistrust   Doubt / Shame   Splitting /   Competition
of   Lack of Confidence Narcissistic / Self Image
Parent Excessive   Borderline   Relationships
       Dependence   Intimacy

influences as well as a component of the family system of codependency as the system serves to maintain the addiction process.

Many theorists have examined the process of early development of the individual in terms of attachment, individuation, and separation, all necessary to achieve differentiation (autonomy, independence). Figure 2 depicts: (a) Early Stages in Normal Development adapted from Mahler (1975); Freud (1966), and Erikson (1959), and (B) Developmental Problems Contributing to Potential Addiction (the result of difficulties in progressing through the developmental stages). It is generally accepted that by age three an individual has negotiated the stages necessary to form attachments, separate from the primary caretaker, begin developing a sense of identity in the separation/individuation process, deal with ''age appropriate'' frustration, and achieve object constancy (the ability to maintain a mental representation of the parent when not present). Basic to progressing through the stages is the relationship with the primary caretaker(s). Problems are said to occur when parenting is not adequate or ''good enough,'' i.e., overly protective, inconsistent, unavailable, or unresponsive to needs. When caretaking is not adequate individuals may remain overly dependent, exhibit inability to maintain relationships or if attachment has not taken place at all may exhibit autistic or psychotic pathology. Later manifestations may be seen in low self-esteem, problems in identification, poor impulse control, inability to reality test, etc. The latter are frequently seen in individuals who develop dependence on alcohol or drugs. Other problems identified by Freud and Erikson related to early development are the formation of shame and guilt. The writer proposes that the intrapsychic dynamics of the individual resulting from early deprivation in parenting predispose/and or exacerbate the potential for addiction. (Other factors, of course, must be taken into consideration, e.g., biological, neurological, genetic.)

Development of a positive self image requires the individual to move through the stages from symbiosis to separation/individuation and integrate introjected parts of the good and bad parent. If the normal process of development does not occur the individual may be stuck (''fixated'') or regress to an earlier stage of development. During the period of 18 months to 2 1/2 years the child experiences frustration. If this period is successfully completed, frustration tolerance, integrating good and bad aspects of the parent and increasing individuation toward the process of differentiation should occur. If problems occur, intense anger/rage, splitting and other acting out occurs and may serve as a base for later pathology. It is suggested that borderline and narcissistic disorders are said to be problems often emanating from this stage. Borderline and narcissistic disorders have been identified in literature related to addicted individuals (Kosten, 1989; Inman et al., 1985; Wurmser, 1984).

Based on research findings regarding the backgrounds of addicted individuals, deficits in parenting may be said to be related to problems in early development, and consequently influence the potential for addiction. Early development then is seen as instrumental in the course of chemical addiction emanating from early difficulties wherein attachment, individuation, separation and differentiation are thwarted. Behaviors which are seen by professionals working with this population include difficulties in establishing trust, difficulty in establishing or inability in maintaining positive relationships, as well as manifestations of primary defense mechanisms including denial, rationalization, splitting, projection and isolation. These will be described in the next section which discusses individual dynamics as part of codependency.

DYNAMICS OF THE INDIVIDUAL CONTRIBUTING TO CHEMICAL DEPENDENCY

A model depicting Development and Maintenance of Addiction: Individual and Family Interaction is presented in Figure 3. The four stage model identifies levels of interaction between the family and the individual in the development and maintenance of addiction. The stages are: (I) Family Influences/Intergenerational Processes; (II) Early Psychological Development; (III) Individual Addiction Process; and (IV) Family Codependency Components. Once addiction has developed it becomes a focal point for the complementary interactions between the individual and family which support the addiction.

The previous section provided an overview of early psychological development of the individual and potential problems in addiction. As the individual progresses through life, the dynamics estab-

18 Chemical Dependency: Theoretical Approaches and Strategies

FIGURE 3. Development and Maintenance of Addiction: Individual and Family Interaction

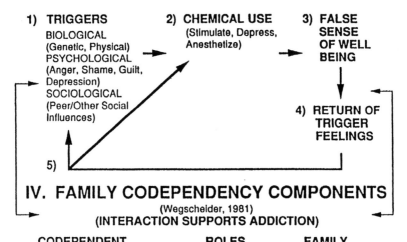

I. FAMILY INFLUENCES/ INTERGENERATIONAL PROCESSES
GENETIC
PSYCHOLOGICAL
LEARNED BEHAVIORS
CODEPENDENCY PATTERNS

II. EARLY PSYCHOLOGICAL DEVELOPMENT
(See Figure 2)

III. INDIVIDUAL ADDICTION PROCESS

1) TRIGGERS
BIOLOGICAL
(Genetic, Physical)
PSYCHOLOGICAL
(Anger, Shame, Guilt, Depression)
SOCIOLOGICAL
(Peer/Other Social Influences)

2) CHEMICAL USE
(Stimulate, Depress, Anesthetize)

3) FALSE SENSE OF WELL BEING

4) RETURN OF TRIGGER FEELINGS

5)

IV. FAMILY CODEPENDENCY COMPONENTS
(Wegscheider, 1981)
(INTERACTION SUPPORTS ADDICTION)

CODEPENDENT CHARACTERISTICS	ROLES	FAMILY RULES
Investment of Self Esteem In Others; Control of Others	HERO	DON'T FEEL
	SCAPEGOAT	DON'T TALK
Responsible for Meeting Others Needs Over Own	LOST CHILD	DON'T TRUST
	MASCOT	
Anxiety Around Boundary, Intimacy & Separation Issues	ENABLER	DON'T THINK
		DON'T CHANGE
Enmeshed in Relation to Chemical Dependency		

lished in early development continue to impact intrapersonal and interpersonal functioning. This section describes the dynamic components which contribute to development and maintenance of addiction. Affective components presented include shame, guilt, anger, and capacity for intimacy. Defense mechanisms commonly related to addiction including denial, rationalization, minimalization and projection are also described.

Affective Components

Anger, shame, guilt, and depression become part of an individual's repertoire of responses to external and internal stimuli, the potential for their expression established as part of early development and necessarily dependent on the caretakers in the environment. As such they become part of the process of addiction and may serve as triggers of substance use, while also serving to maintain the use of the substance as the desired effect of the chemical wears off. As chemical use continues, a process of reinforcement occurs in response to physiological needs, psychological needs, and social experiences, each of which may serve as a trigger for further use. The individual's sense of self and ego functioning are said to play a role in the addiction process; deficiency in self and poor ego functioning have been suggested as motivating the use of chemicals as an attempt at feeling better (Khantzian, 1977; Levin, 1987). A brief description of anger, depression, shame, guilt and intimacy follows.

Anger. Anger occurs as a reaction to felt resentment and injustice, and occurs in all families. In functional families, there is an *energy outlet* which encourages appropriate resolution and growth of the individual members. In families characterized by addiction, expression of anger is often discouraged and may be suppressed (Rosellini and Worden, 1985). Where there is no appropriate outlet, or the individual is not able to handle the intensity the anger may escalate to rage. Kohut (1971) describes a "void" in feelings of self which may occur in addiction and prompt regression to "archaic narcissism" and rage.

Depression. Depression is described as a state that develops in response to loss or "narcissistic deprivations" (Wurmser, 1974).

Reactions vary from sadness to suicide. Addiction has been cited by Gaylin (1983) as warding off depression. In chemical addiction it is essential to know the difference between depression that is chemically induced or one that is a mental disorder. It is only possible to know the difference when an individual has been abstinent for a period of time; opinions vary regarding the length of time an individual must be abstinent for an accurate diagnosis to be made but usually varies from two to several weeks depending on chemical use.

Shame and Guilt. Shame and guilt have been identified as feelings which are related to the development of chemical dependency as well as the dynamics which affect the individual and family (Bradshaw, 1988; Potter-Efron, 1987; Wurmser, 1974). Potter-Efron defines shame as a "failure of being, a painful emotional sense of falling short that attacks the core of self concept"; guilt is defined as a "failure of doing . . . telling the individual that he has done or is thinking something wrong, immoral, or unethical." Both are described as having roots in childhood which surface as pain during the development of chemical dependency. In an effort to protect oneself from the emotional pain of shame, defenses such as denial, withdrawal, grandiosity and rage surface. Defenses against guilt include obsessive thought patterns, paranoid thinking, intellectualization and rationalization.

Intimacy. Intimacy has been defined as "a qualitative relationship between two or more people in which individuals have the ability to express feelings in a meaningful and constructive manner in a way that is mutually acceptable and leads to psychological well-being of the individuals involved" (Coleman, 1987). The potential for intimacy begins in the early development of the individual in relationship to parental figures; families characterized by chemical dependency commonly exhibit intimacy dysfunction (see Early Psychological Development, Figure 2). Chemical dependency is often substituted for the inability to have a relationship with another person; the chemical becomes a substitute object in the relationship (Covington and Beckett, 1988).

While the painful feelings of anger, rage, guilt, and shame are related to addiction, they also evoke defensive reactions in individuals and family members. A description of defense mechanisms common to addiction are presented in the next section.

Defense Mechanisms

The use of defense mechanisms as they pertain to addiction have been discussed by various writers (Bean, 1981; Kaufman, 1985; Zimberg et al., 1985) and include denial, rationalization, minimization, splitting and projection. Defense mechanisms serve to protect the individual and the family from confronting the chemical use. As part of the family system, defenses help to maintain the homeostasis of addiction.

Anna Freud (1966) defined defense mechanisms as the way in which the ego responds to pain and anxiety from external and internal sources in controlling impulses and affects. Defenses have also been identified as warding off narcissistic injuries which attack the self-perception of the individual (Bean, 1981; Wallace, 1989; Wurmser, 1977) and thus support the continued use of the addictive substance. In addition the use of drugs as defenses against feelings of rage, hurt, shame and loneliness is suggested by Wurmser (1977) and Khantzian (1977).

As the individual exhibits defensive reactions, family members respond in complementary ways (consistent with rules related to communication, feelings and intimacy), often exhibiting similar defenses in communication patterns and roles which support the system (Kaufman and Kaufmann, 1979). The reaction of the family during active addiction often results in denying and rationalizing the behaviors of the individual to friends, employers, etc., ultimately resulting in isolation of both the addicted individual and family members. The following definitions of the defenses identified are provided:

Denial. Denial is a defense attempting to avoid unpleasant reality (Campbell, 1981) and has also been described as a means to "justify, hide or protect drinking, block treatment and deny responsibility for the consequences of behavior" (Bean, 1981).

Rationalization and Minimization. Rationalization and minimization are offered as variations of denial. Rationalization is an attempt to justify the addictive behavior, e.g., "Everyone else was drinking." Minimization is an attempt to downplay the use, e.g., "Only two drinks, one joint."

Splitting. Splitting is described as a defense against ambivalent feelings toward an individual (Campbell, 1981), e.g., an addicted individual exhibits strong feelings which idealize or denigrate someone. This is characteristic of "all or nothing thinking" often evidenced in addiction.

Projection. Projection is described as an "unconscious throwing out upon another the ideas or impulses (usually considered undesirable) that belong to oneself" (Campbell, 1981), e.g., an alcoholic blaming spouse for his/her drinking and the codependent spouse blaming the alcoholic for not pursuing his/her personal or professional goals. Wallace (1989) discusses defenses as a result of chemical addiction and suggests that the individual develops a preferred defense structure. He further suggests that the preferred defense structure may be used by professionals in working positively toward the process of recovery. Wallace identifies assimilative projection as part of active drinking as well as recovery. In active alcoholism, the drinker identifies with his/her drinking friends while in recovery there is positive identification with members of self-help groups such as AA, NA.

In summary, the development of addiction is presented as a systemic interaction between the individual and the family. It is suggested that codependency interactions evidenced in dysfunctional roles and rules reinforce the individual dynamics as part of the addictive cycle and in turn maintain family dysfunctional dynamics supporting addiction.

DISCUSSION

Chemical addiction of the individual has been discussed by looking at the early development and family codependency interactions which play a part in developing and maintaining the homeostasis of chemical dependency in the family system.

Assessment of chemical dependency in the individual and family is suggested. This process includes: (1) assessing the chemical use by the individual and family; (2) obtaining individual development and family history to understand the current dynamics in relation to intergenerational patterns of addiction; and (3) identifying current patterns of codependency including roles of family members and rules of communication supporting the chemical use.

Intervention is suggested at the individual and family system level with a focus on changing behaviors and communications related to and supportive of abstinence. Interventions are focused on the intradynamics of the individual (feelings, defensive reactions) and the family interactions (roles, rules, boundaries) supporting chemical use. The use of self-help groups such as AA, NA, and Al-Anon are instrumental in promoting abstinence and recovery.

Clinicians should be trained in understanding the development and maintenance of addiction from a multilevel perspective including individual, family and environmental influences. The following tenets are offered as a basic to working with individuals and family members:

1. The development of addiction of the individual is related to early family influences, especially the primary caretaker(s).
2. The individual and the family interact as part of the psychological and social system supporting addiction.
3. Intergenerational incidence of addiction is likely to support the continuation of addiction through learned behaviors and interactions of family members.
4. Working with families characterized by addiction is a practical approach in working with the individual, couple and/or other subsets of the family system.
5. Working with individuals and family members should be conducted within the broader biopsychosocial model recognizing disease, genetic, psychological and social systems influences.
6. Ongoing assessment of the addicted individual and significant family members should be conducted at each stage of recovery.
7. The use of self-help groups is recommended as basic to abstinence and recovery.

CONCLUSION

This chapter provides a framework for understanding family systems and chemical addiction. Background on the history of family systems and related research supports the use of family systems as an intervention in chemical addiction. Family systems components and their application to addiction are reviewed including homeostasis and codependency interactions in maintaining addiction. The importance of early development of the individual is discussed and the dynamics of the individual in the family system is presented. The overall goal of abstinence and recovery in chemical addiction is suggested to be a function of ongoing assessment of, and intervention with the individual and family system.

NOTE

1. Chemical dependency is used to denote alcohol and other drug addiction.

REFERENCES

Allen, D.M. (1988). *Unifying individual and family therapies*. San Francisco, CA: Jossey-Bass Pubs.

Barry, K.L., Fleming, M.F. (1990). Family cohesion, expressiveness and conflict in alcoholic families. *British Journal of Addictions, 85*: 81-86.

Bean, M., Khantzian, E., Mack, J., Vaillant, G. & Zinberg, N. (1981). *Dynamic approaches to the understanding and treatment of alcoholism*. New York: Free Press.

Bepko, C. & Krestan, J. (1985). *The responsibility trap: A blueprint for treating the alcoholic family*. New York: Free Press.

Billings, A., Kessler, M., Gomberg, E., & Weiner, S. (1979). Marital conflict resolution of alcoholic and non-alcoholics during sobriety and experimental drinking. *Journal of Studies on Alcohol. 3*:183-195.

Blaine, J.D., & Julius, D.A. (1977). Psychodynamics of Drug Dependency. *NIDA Research Monograph No. 12* Washington, D.C.: Government Printing Office.

Bowen, M. (1974). Alcoholism as viewed through family systems and family psychotherapy. *Annals of N.Y. Academy of Sciences.* 223:115-122.

_____. (1978). *Family therapy in clinical practice*. New York: Jason Aronson.

Bradshaw, J. (1988). *Bradshaw On The Family. A Revolutionary Way of Self-Discovery*. Deerfield Beach, FL: Health Communications, Inc.

Brown, S. (1985). *Treating the Alcoholic*. New York: John Wiley and Sons, Inc.

Campbell, R.J. (1981). *Psychiatric Dictionary*, 5th Ed. New York: Oxford University Press, Inc.

Carruth, B., & Mendenhall, W. (1989). *Co-dependency: Issues in Treatment and Recovery*. New York: The Haworth Press Inc.

Chaudron, C.D., & Wilkinson, D.A. (eds.) (1988). *Theories on Alcoholism*. Addiction Research Foundation. Toronto, Canada.

Coleman, E. (1987). Chemical dependency and intimacy dysfunction. *Journal of Chemical Dependency Treatment*. Vol. 1, No. 1. New York: The Haworth Press Inc.

Covington, S. & Beckett, L. (1988). *Leaving the Enchanted Forest, the Path From Relationship Addiction to Intimacy*. New York: Harper & Row, Publishers.

Davis, D., Berenson, D., Steinglass, P., & Davis, S. (1974). The adaptive consequences of drinking. *Psychiatry*, *37*:209-215.

Eells, M.A.W. (1986). Interventions with alcoholics and their families. *Journal Psychiatric/Mental Health Nursing*. Vol. 21, No. 3: 493-504.

Erikson, E. (1959). Growth and crises of the healthy personality. *Psychological Issues*. Vol. 1, No. 1, Monograph 1, New York: International University Press.

_____. (1959). *Identity and the Life Cycle*. New York: W.W. Norton and Company.

Fishman, H.C. (1988). *Treating Troubled Adolescents, A Family Therapy Approach*. New York: Basic Books, Inc.

Freud, A. (1966). *The Ego and the Mechanisms of Defense*. New York: International University Press, Inc.

_____. (1966). *Normality and Pathology in Childhood: Assessments of Development. The Writings of Anna Freud*. Vol. 6, New York: International University Press.

Gaylin, W. (1983). *Psychodynamic Understanding of Depression*. New York: Jason Aronson.

Goodwin. (1984). Studies of familial alcoholism: A review. *Journal of Clinical Psychiatry*, *45*(12, Sec. 2): 14-17.

Goodwin, D. (1971). Is alcoholism hereditary? *Archetypes of General Psychiatry*. 25:545-549.

Grichting, N.L., & Barber, J.G. (1989). The impact of quality of family life on drug consumption. *The International Journal of Addictions*. 24(10), 963-971.

Guerin, P.J. (1976). *Family Therapy Theory and Practice*. New York: Gardner Press, Inc.

Harburg, E., DiFrancesco, W., Webster, D.W., Gleiberman, L., & Schork, A. (1990). Familial transmission of alcohol use: II. Imitation of and aversion to parent drinking (1960) by adult offspring (1977). *Journal of Studies on Alcohol*. Vol. 51, No. 3: 245-256.

Inman, D., Bascue, L., & Skoloda, T. (1985). Identification of borderline personality disorders among substance abuse inpatients. *Journal of Substance Abuse Treatment*, 2:229-232.

Jacob, T. (1982). *Alcoholism: A Family Interactive Perspective.* University of Nebraska Press. Vol. 34:159-206.

Jacob, T., Ritchey, D., & Cuitkovic, J. (1981). Communication styles of alcoholics and families when drinking and not drinking. *Journal of Studies on Alcohol, 42*:466-482.

Kaij, L. (1960). Alcoholism in twins: studies on the etiology and sequels of abuse of alcohol. *Stockholm: Almquist & Wiksell.*

Kaufman, E. (1985). Family systems and family therapy of substance abuse: An overview of two decades of research and clinical experience. *International Journal of the Addictions, 20*(6 & 7):897-916.

Kaufman, E., & Kaufmann, P. (1979). *Family Therapy of Drug and Alcohol Abuse.* New York: Gardner Press, Inc.

Khantzian, E. (1977). The ego, the self, and opiate addiction: theoretical and treatment considerations. In Blaine, J. & Julius, D. *Psychodynamics of Drug Dependence.* NIDA Research Monograph 12. Washington, D.C.: U.S. Department of Health, Education & Welfare.

Kirschner, D.A., & Kirschner, S. (1986). *Comprehensive Family Therapy, An Integration of Systemic and Psychodynamic Treatment Models.* New York: Brunner/Mazel Pubs.

Kohut, H. (1971). *The Analysis of the Self.* New York: International University Press.

Kosten, T.A., Kosten, T.R., & Rounsaville, B.J. (1984). Personality disorders in opiate addicts show prognostic specificity. *Journal of Substance Abuse Treatment.* Vol. 6: 163-168.

Lawson, G., Peterson, J., & Lawson, A. (1983). *Alcoholism and the Family.* Rockville, MD: Aspen Systems Corporation.

Levin, J.D. (1987). *Treatment of Alcoholism and Other Addictions. A Self Psychology Approach.* New Jersey: Jason Aronson, Inc.

Levin, J.D. (1990). *Alcoholism: A Biopsychosocial Approach.* New York: Hemisphere Publishing Corporation.

McGrady, B.S., Noell, N.E., Abrams, D., Stout, R.L., Nelson, H.F., & Hay, W.M. (1986). Comparative effectiveness of three types of spouse involvement in outpatient behavioral alcoholism treatment. *Journal Studies on Alcohol, 47*(6), 459-467.

Mahler, M.S., Pine, F., & Bergman, A. (1975). *The Psychological Birth of the Infant.* New York: Basic Books, Inc.

Mapes, B.E., Johnson, R.A., & Sandler, K.R. (1985). The alcoholic family: diagnosis and treatment. *Alcoholism Treatment Quarterly.* Vol. 1(4): 67-83. New York: The Haworth Press Inc.

Miller, L. (1990). Neuropsychodynamics of alcoholism and addiction: personality, psychopathology, and cognitive style. *Journal of Substance Abuse Treatment.* Vol. 7:31-49.

Minuchin, S. (1974). *Families and Family Therapy.* Cambridge, MA: Harvard University Press.

Minuchin, S., & Fishman, H.C. (1981). *Family Therapy Techniques.* Cambridge, MA: Harvard University Press.

O'Farrell, T.J. (1989). Marital and family therapy in alcoholism treatment. *Journal of Substance Abuse Treatment.* Vol. 6:23-29.

Pandina, R.J., & Johnson, V. (1990). Serious alcohol and drug problems among adolescents with a family history of alcoholism. *Journal of Studies on Alcohol.* Vol. 51, No. 3: 278-282.

Paolino, J., & McGrady, B. (1977). *The Alcoholic Marriage: Alternative Perspectives.* New York: Grune and Stratton.

Potter-Efron, R., (1987). Guilt and Shame. *Journal of Chemical Dependency Treatment.* New York: The Haworth Press Inc.

Potter-Efron, R., & Potter-Efron, P. (1989). *Letting Go of Shame.* New York: Harper & Row, Pub.

Rosselini, G., & Worden, M. (1985). *Of Course You're Angry.* Center City, MN: Hazelden.

Stanton, D., & Todd. (1982). *The Family Therapy of Drug Abuse and Addiction.* New York: The Guilford Press.

Wurmser, L. (1984). More respect for the neurotic process: comments on the problem of narcissism in severe psychopathology, especially the addictions. *Journal of Substance Abuse Treatment.* Vol. 1:37-45.

Zimberg, S., Wallace, J., & Blume, S. (eds.). (1985). *Practical Approaches to Alcoholism Psychotherapy.* New York: Plenum Publishing Corporation.

Zucker, R.A., & Gomberg, E.L. (1986). Etiology of alcoholism reconsidered. The case for the biopsychosocial process. *American Psychologist* July. 783-793.

Structural and Strategic Family Therapy Techniques: Application to Chemically Dependent Families

Donna Richardson, ACSW, CAC

SUMMARY. This article provides an overview of the theoretical framework for the use of selected structural and strategic techniques for treatment of alcohol and drug affected families in inpatient and outpatient settings when families present problems in addition to chemical dependency. Techniques are illustrated with case materials. An argument is made for the flexible application of both the theory and the techniques, taking into consideration the family, the therapist and the setting.

Family therapy in the field of addiction treatment is no longer new. There is an array of material, ranging from self-help tapes to scientific journal articles, which use the underpinnings of systems theory to view the family not as the cause of alcoholism but as directly involved in sustaining the addiction and critical to the process of changing the addiction. It would appear that seeing addiction as a family problem has not only aided treatment, but has brought the problem out of the closet and into the book aisle of our supermarkets.

The tradition of family therapy reaches back to general systems theory to the notion of interdependence. Betty Carter and Monica McGoldrick (1980) write:

Donna Richardson is a clinician at the Family Relations Center, Community Mental Health Center at Piscataway, University of Medicine and Dentistry of New Jersey. She maintains a private practice in Metuchen, NJ.

29

The assumptions of family systems therapy are based on the idea that the family is the primary, and except in rare circumstances, the most powerful emotional system we ever belong to, which shapes and continues to determine the course and outcome of our lives. As in any system, relationships and functioning (physical, social, and emotional) are interdependent, and a change in one part of the system is followed by compensatory change in other parts of the system. Such primary impact makes the family our greatest potential resource as well as our greatest potential source of stress.

Philip Guerin (1976) outlines four "orientations" in the family therapy field that have arisen from the emphasis on the family as a system: (1) general systems, (2) structural family therapy, (3) strategic family therapy, and (4) Bowenian family therapy. To this list, feminist family therapy might be added.

The purpose of this paper is to describe the uses of the strategic and structural family therapy orientations of the family systems approach. In doing so, a cautionary note must first be sounded. The isolated use of any single family treatment orientation is inadvisable. The author's experience through clinical practice in various settings has been that an eclectic application of the various approaches to treating families is necessary. Clients care little about the "schools" from which interventions are derived—they value that which "works," and respond to techniques that show respect for the reality of their lives.

In recent years, interest in the treatment of addiction has grown dramatically as addiction is recognized as pervasive and dynamically related to other presenting problems. Yet the problems of addiction are in many respects unique, requiring special understanding and experience. Although addiction treatment specialists are increasingly sought as consultants—formal and informal—to other therapists who seek assistance with chemically dependant clients, it must be recognized that many traditional approaches to treatment are inappropriate to the context of addiction. As Bepko and Krestan (1985) have said:

. . . addiction takes on a life of its own within the individual that, although affecting and affected by the system, cannot be entirely addressed by shifting the system. The relationship between the addict and the drug needs to be disrupted as well. Systemic change is a necessary, but not sufficient, response to an addiction.

By becoming conversant in the language of family systems — and by developing skills in these techniques — addiction specialists can increase their appropriate use by themselves and their more generalist colleagues.

STRUCTURAL FAMILY THERAPY

Salvator Minuchin is most closely associated with the structural orientation. His outline of characteristics present in the well functioning family provides directions for change in family dynamics. Lynn Hoffman's *Foundations of Family Therapy* (1981) provides a helpful synopsis of Minuchin's characteristics of a "healthy" family. A healthy family has clearly marked boundaries between individuals and subgroups or subsystems. There is privacy, there is individual integrity, and there is a differentiation of family roles. Family members see each other as distinct human beings, though they also feel a connection to each other. While individuals experience a sense of rootedness in the family, there is also space and nourishment for each member to grow. Important to the structural model is the concept of family subsystems. A healthy family contains an adult subsystem functioning primarily in a leadership role. This subsystem has privacy, assumes responsibility and exerts power. The subsystem need not take the traditional form of husband/wife, but can be creatively formed and maintained by one adult orchestrating resources outside of the family unit in support of the leadership function. In addition there is a clear boundary between the parental subsystem and the subsystem of the children with the child being the recipient of direction and rules, not the rule-maker.

For example, when a mother establishes the child's mealtimes, clear boundaries between her role and that of her child are maintained even though the meals are provided by another caregiver. While the boundary should be clear, it need not be rigid, depending on the developmental level of family members.

Sibling boundaries in healthy families are clear as well. Power and responsibility commensurate with the child's age and ability, when enforced by the leader subsystem, make for consistency, order and predictability — all conducive to human growth and development.

The chemically dependent family stands in contrast to the healthy family prototyped by Minuchin. Claudia Bepko (1989) has outlined the following dynamics as characteristic of chemically dependent families: (1) Rigidity or violation of boundaries; (2) inability to resolve conflict; (3) detouring of parental conflict through the addict; (4) enmeshment; and (5) overprotectiveness.

Successful application of the techniques of structural family therapy would address boundary issues, triangulation as well as the lack of individuation present in chemically dependent families. Duncan Stanton (1979), who has evaluated the use of family therapy techniques in the treatment of chemical dependence, characterizes structural family therapy techniques as focusing on five issues: (1) Patterns of interaction within the family; (2) communication within session influencing these patterns directly and actively; (3) homework outside the session; (4) setting boundaries; and (5) restructuring the family and reinforcing generational boundaries. He concludes that "the ability to be active is a cornerstone of structural therapy."

Such goals as "changing the family subsystem membership," "changing the distance between subsystems" and "changing the hierarchical relationships of the family" are particularly relevant for families where the addicted parent is disengaged and may be more affiliated with the sibling subsystem than the parental one (Minuchin, 1981).

As the structural therapist enters the family system, attempting to intervene and to make way for change, these important questions are to be considered: "To whom does he (the therapist) speak? Who is allowed to speak? Whom does he elevate? Whom does he challenge? Which persons does he bring together? Which does he push apart? With whom does he make a coalition? With whom does he not? It is by such moves that the therapist begins to restructure the relationship system in the family, and to alter the context that supposedly nourishes the symptom," (Hoffman, 1981).

Michael Elkin's book *Under the Influence* (1984) provides a lengthy illustration of his initial failure to consider important structural questions about a chemically dependent family in treatment. After a crisis occurred in the family, Elkin illustrates how he then employed structural techniques to intervene successfully.

Structural interventions need not be done by the therapist directly. Referrals to 12-step programs can be viewed as structural interventions in that involvement in such programs appears to have the potential to reinforce boundaries, to promote individuation, and deal with enmeshment. When each family member establishes a niche in his or her own 12-step program, affiliation can be provided which addresses the disengagement of the addict in the family. Equally important, investment in 12 step programs serves as an ally to the therapist in unbalancing the system.

In a similar way, the structural family therapist can use referral to intensive day or residential treatment facilities to unbalance the system and to reinforce boundaries. Intensive program referrals can be framed in various positive ways to the disengaged addict.

STRATEGIC FAMILY THERAPY

The writings of Jay Haley, Paul Watzlawick and John Weakland, sometimes referred to as the "Palo Alto Group," are considered to be most illustrative of the strategic approach to family therapy. The strategic school can be characterized by the following features:

1. The presenting problem is explored in detail. Lynn Hoffman (1981) notes the important questions asked by the strategic family therapist:
   - What is the problem?
   - Who did what the last time it happened?
   - When is it likely to occur?
   - When did it first appear?
2. The therapist is concerned with the presenting problem only.
3. Problems are seen as self-reinforcing cycles; e.g., a problem in living creates the context which reinforces its continuation.

The techniques of strategic family therapy involve direct instruction, sometimes called "prescriptions." Prescriptions will take the form of techniques such as reframing (or positive relabeling) the problem. The strategic family therapist may use the technique of "paradox," in which prescriptions seemingly contradictory to common sense are given to the client. For example, the therapist may paradoxically prescribe that the cure lies in doing more of the same, in an attempt to magnify its dysfunctionality. Alternatively, the mirror behavior may be prescribed in an attempt to reverse the behavior. Or, the therapist may "provide the family with a worse alternative," setting up two choices, one impossible and the other difficult but conceivable.

Some techniques of strategic therapy seem inappropriate to the chemically dependant family. For example, it makes little sense to instruct an addict to double his or her usage. Likewise, suggesting that the mate (or child's parent) should mirror the substance abuse is counterproductive.

This is not to say that strategic methods have no application. Bepko and Krestan illustrate the use of strategic techniques with paradoxical flavor in *The Responsibility Trap* (1985). In working with the much-heralded denial resources of chemically dependent individuals and family members, Bepko and Krestan (1985) suggest:

> the clinician should continue to convey information about alcoholism at the same time that he restrains the family, spouse, or drinker from making hasty decisions or from moving into action too quickly.

APPLICATIONS

Throughout the family therapy literature there is reference to the therapist's personal style, family of origin issues, belief systems and values. There is a consensus that family therapy is an art. Much of the work is creatively spontaneous in which the therapist as a person mixes with the therapist as a helper.

Skill development is crucial in the family therapy training process. Just as crucial is the personal journey, taken collaboratively with teachers, supervisors, colleagues and co-therapists. This will be especially true for therapists with an interest in treatment of chemically dependent families, for many will find among their clients, roles they themselves have played in their own families.

The therapist will be choosing techniques that make more flexible and effective the role-taking of the members of the family. Truly one of the wonders of this work is that in real life, with real families, in real sessions, therapists mix and match techniques. No pure form of a given school is required for effective family therapy.

The following case illustrations are offered in abbreviated form with precautions taken for preserving the confidentiality of the families. The use of structural and strategic methods are illustrated within the broader context of family therapy.

The Robbins Family

Michelle Robbins was referred for individual therapy to the community mental health center unit specializing in sexual abuse by her stepfather's therapist, following depletion of family insurance and other financial resources. Michelle, 19, had received, in chronological order, family treatment with both parents, adolescent inpatient alcohol and drug rehabilitation incorporating a 12-step program, and individual psychotherapy with a private therapist who worked closely with her stepfather's therapist. Michelle's presenting problem was her mother's difficulty with her choice of boyfriend. Her parents noted her preference for violent, alcohol troubled males and felt her relationships were having a negative impact on their two younger children, Mary, age 12, and Sam, age 9.

Other relevant information obtained at intake included the history of Michelle's sexual abuse from ages 9-16 years, by her stepfather. Her introduction to marijuana use by her stepfather became an integral feature of the sexual abuse dynamics: he was her dealer. The sexual abuse was disclosed by Michelle during her 60 day inpatient treatment for marijuana and alcoholic dependence, and cocaine abuse. There were no recurrences of the sexual abuse following Michelle's disclosure. Mr. Robbins was arrested, freed on bail, and subsequently pled guilty in exchange for a probation sentence. His probation sentence conditions required psychotherapy with a specialist in sexual dysfunction. There was no requirement for drug or alcohol monitoring, despite Mr. Robbins earlier involvement. The legal system and child protective service system interventions kept the family in crisis for over one year.

Michelle agreed to come in for individual treatment but refused to enter therapy with any members of her family due to previous experiences.

Assessment with Michelle determined she had discontinued her involvement with 12-step programs and was engaging in episodic drinking. It soon became apparent that at the same time she went on drinking binges, she also engaged in outrageous behavior with her boyfriend. These episodes included trying to run him down with her car, for example. Michelle herself saw a connection between her drinking and her episodes. Though highly verbal, she was strikingly muddled about the events of her life.

Making use of the strategic notion of focus on the presenting problem, I asked many detailed questions about her boyfriend, and her behavior with him as well as her understanding of her family's objections to him. Two things became clear as we explored this material: (1) Her boyfriend and her stepfather had much in common, behaviorally; and (2) the boyfriend served as a powerful means to express her rage at her parents. I made reference in paradoxical fashion from time to time to both the sexual abuse and her drinking, cautioning her to wait until the right time to work on. issues of a more historical nature than the immediate problem — her boyfriend.

Maybe we "detailed" the boyfriend to death. She decided on her own he wasn't very appealing. Michelle broke up with him and asked if we could talk about the sexual abuse. I told her we could, but cautioned that we probably wouldn't make much progress since she seems to still wish to drink. I predicted her drinking would get worse since work on the sexual abuse issue sometimes had that effect. Having a specialty in alcoholism, I told her, I was the last person in the world who would want her to do something that would make her drinking worse. She volunteered to return to A.A. as a safeguard. I also advised that involving her family in her treatment was crucial to its success.

We discussed what might happen if her family came in. Her little brother might find out about the abuse, and become depressed like her sister had when protective service workers had interviewed her regarding the abuse. Her parents might separate. It might be too hard on her mom. In the end, Michelle made the decision to invite her mother, and her two siblings to treatment but to exclude her father who had not yet been able to take sufficient responsibility for the abuse, and who had separated from the family. His individual treatment continued per the court order.

I switched to a more structural approach as the other family members joined Michelle. I assisted Michelle's mom in telling, with Michelle's help, the younger children the secret of the abuse. (My throat still tightens when I recall Sam's response: "Thank you, Mommy, for bringing me here. I thought Dad just didn't like me very much because he always wanted to be alone with Michelle.") We created and observed boundaries by limiting the information regarding the abuse to age-appropriate discussion of touching, bodies, and drug abuse. The younger children were able to explain to Michelle that her drinking hurt them the way their father's drug abuse and other behavior had hurt them all.

The next phase of treatment called for reinforcement of boundaries and individual growth. Mrs. Robbins returned to Al-Anon, joined a mother's group for mothers of incest victims, and continued family therapy. Our sessions focused on hierarchy, roles and boundaries in the family, as they reorganized themselves around family maintenance tasks. Michelle, now 20 years old, joined an adult survivor's group, and experienced validation in a way that resulted in seemingly miraculous clarity of thought expression. Her abstinence from alcohol was framed as a reward to herself; her chemical dependence was viewed as an aspect of the abuse which she was now empowered to prevent.

The Adaminski Family

Mike Adaminski, a psychologist and the married father of two, was referred "to discuss his drinking," by a mutual colleague. He wasn't really sure his drinking was a problem; he'd had such a complicated life with so many significant early losses. Yet his children, Susie and Teddy, were getting older and were making comments about his drinking. His wife, herself recovering from prescription drug dependence, didn't seem troubled about his use of alcohol, and she had been through rehabilitation and knew a lot, he thought, about dependence.

Mike and I chatted for the first three sessions about the patterns, tracking the details of his drinking. He told me of the small bottles he could easily hide so that the children wouldn't see. I was careful to avoid diagnostic labels, such as "alcoholic." And I was deliberately casual — careful to avoid interfering with his own identification process. We spoke in terms of what would it mean if he did have a problem with alcohol.

After the third session, as Mike pulled out of the parking lot, I saw him drinking from one of the little, easy-to-hide bottles. It was time for what David Treadway (1987) calls a "controlled drinking contract." In our next session, Mike agreed to drink every other day but to maintain the existing pattern in other respects. We began to discuss what it would mean to be alcoholic. He wanted to discuss available treatment options, but I said we were jumping the gun. I also directed Mike to bring his wife and children next time, telling him that they might prove useful in helping him decide whether alcohol was really a problem or not. Mike wasn't able to maintain the contract.

After a few more sessions, Mike decided a nationally known inpatient program some distance away would work best for him. He made the call. I advised him that he might find himself needing to drink as he anticipated the separation from his family, and that he might interpret his need to drink as confirmation that he had made the right decision. Besides, drinking up to his admission might even be recommended, since it might be physically unsafe for him to attempt withdrawal without medical supervision. He completed inpatient treatment, returned home and has maintained his sobriety.

CONCLUSION

This article has provided an illustration of the techniques of structural and strategic family therapy with chemically dependent families. The rationale and methods of these techniques have been described, and two case illustrations have been provided. It has been argued that strict application of these techniques may not always be warranted with the chemically dependent. However, these proven methods can be adapted flexibly to serve as effective intervention approaches with families troubled by chemical dependency.

BIBLIOGRAPHY

Bepko, C. (1989). Disorders of power: Women and addiction in the family. In ed. McGoldrick, M. Anderson, CM, Walsh, F. *Women in families: A framework for family therapy*. New York: W.W. Norton & Co.

Bepko, C. with Krestan, J. (1985). *The responsibility trap*. New York: The Free Press.

Berenson, D. (1976). "Alcohol and the family system" in P. Guerin (Ed.) *Family therapy*. New York: Gardner Press.

Black, C. (1982). *It will never happen to me*. Denver: Medical Administration Company.

Carter, E., & McGoldrick, M. (1980). *The family life cycle: A framework for family therapy*. New York: Gardner Press.

Elkin, M. (1984). *Families under the influence*. New York: W.W. Norton & Co.

Haley, J. (1986). *Uncommon therapy: The psychiatric techniques of Milton H. Erickson, MD*. New York: W.W. Norton & Co.

Hoffman, L. (1981). *Foundations of family therapy*. New York: Basic Books.

Kaufman, E., & Kaufman, P.N. (Eds.). (1979). *Family therapy of drug and alcohol abuse*. New York: Gardner Press, Inc.

Minuchin, S., & Fishman, H.C. (1981). *Family therapy techniques*. Cambridge, MA: Harvard University Press.

Treadway, D. (1987). "The Ties that Bind." *The Family Networker. July/August Issue*. Washington, DC: The Family Therapy Network.

Psychodynamics and Family Systems: A Model for Chemical Addiction Counseling

Eileen B. Isaacson, EdD, ACSW, CAC

SUMMARY. This chapter provides a model for counseling, using Psychodynamics and Family Systems (Structural, Strategic and Bowen Theories) in working with addicted individuals and family members. Case material is used to demonstrate the practical application of the model.

INTRODUCTION

The use of psychodynamics and family systems as a combined approach to chemical addiction counseling is increasing as both perspectives are viewed as complementary (Kaufman, 1985; Zimberg et al., 1985; Bradshaw, 1988). The following assumptions are provided as a foundation in working with the intrapsychic model of psychodynamics and interpersonal family systems model:

1. The development of chemical dependence[1] is a function of biological (genetic/disease), psychological (early development, learned behaviors), and sociological (family, peers, social) factors, all of which are important in working with addiction (Levin, 1990).
2. Counseling assessment and intervention to promote abstinence and recovery, should include psychodynamics of the

Eileen B. Isaacson is Director of the Brunswik Counseling Group & Training Institute in New Jersey. She is a New Jersey licensed Marriage and Family and Certified Alcoholism Counselor. Correspondence may be sent to the author at 7 Riley Road, Morganville, NJ 07751.

41

individual (Wurmser, 1974; Bean and Zinberg, 1981) as well as interaction with the family.

3. Psychodynamic components of addiction include thoughts, affect and behaviors which emanate from early developmental factors. Problems in early psychological development may result in voids in self esteem and fragmented ego structure. Defenses commonly seen in addiction are denial, rationalization, splitting, and grandiosity which serve to protect the self and ego. Alcohol and drugs are used to fill these voids (Kohut, 1971; Levin, 1987).

4. Transference and defense mechanisms are useful to the counselor in working with the client to address issues related to addiction.

5. Ego functions commonly identified as deficient in addicted clients are reality testing, impulse control, primitive defense functioning, and object relations.

6. The role of chemical dependency is central in the individual's life which is often structured around obtaining and using the substance(s).

7. Family members behave during the development and continuation of the addiction process to support the substance use and its homeostatic function within the family.

8. Defense mechanisms such as denial rationalization, minimization, projection, and splitting, are used as part of maintaining the use of the substance by the individual and family members.

9. Family members will engage in defensive behaviors (identified in 8) and roles which support use. Roles typically include enabler, hero, scapegoat, and mascot (Wegscheider, 1981).

10. Communications within and outside the family contribute to the dysfunctional behaviors and social interactions of chemically dependent individuals and family members. Rules of communication encourage not talking about feelings, behaviors, thoughts or the addiction itself; the family in an attempt to "keep the secret" moves toward a closed system isolating itself from the social environment.

11. In an attempt to maintain the homeostasis of the family sys-

tem, problems unrelated to the addiction surface. Problems such as marital conflict and projecting problems onto children who are then identified as the problem are common; these children or the addicted adult are often viewed as scapegoats. Reciprocally, addiction may be presented as a problem which masks other problems.

Basic to working with the individual and family system is an understanding of the dynamics of addiction in the individual and family. The reader is referred to the article, "Chemical Addiction: Individuals and Family Systems," for an explanation of early psychological development and individual and family interaction as related to addiction.

It is suggested that counselors knowledgeable of the dynamics of chemical dependency focus on addressing addictive patterns through on-going assessment and intervention with the individual and family. A model identifying the components of psychodynamics and family systems in chemical addiction counseling is presented in Figure 1 and discussed as it relates to a case.

PSYCHODYNAMICS

Psychodynamics is defined as the mental forces that result from ideas, impulses and emotions interacting for some adaptational purpose; these interactions are shaped by biological and environmental influences and respond to internal and external stimuli (Campbell, 1981). The psychodynamics of addiction refers to the unconscious reactions to conflicts which are described in transference, resistance and defense mechanisms such as denial, projection, splitting, rationalization and minimization. The development of addiction is related to early psychological development (see article, "Chemical Addiction: Individuals and Families," Figure 2), and the use of drugs as a way to "take care of a central defect in his self" . . . "the drug provides him with the self-esteem he does not possess" (Kohut, 1971). In effect, the drug takes the place of the object relationship. Impaired functioning of the ego has been identified by theorists in relation to addiction (Kohut, 1971; Levin, 1987; Wurmser,

FIGURE 1

Psychodynamic & Family Systems Model for Addiction Counseling

OVERALL GOAL: TO CHANGE THINKING, FEELING, AND BEHAVIORAL PATTERNS RELATED TO ADDICTION AND PROMOTE DIFFERENTIATION OF INDIVIDUAL AND FAMILY SYSTEM.

THEORETICAL MODEL	COUNSELOR ROLE	MODEL COMPONENTS COMPONENTS	FOR CHANGE PROMOTE CHANGE THROUGH

I. PSYCHODYNAMIC
Focus:
A) Individual (Intrapsychic)
B) Past as relates to present
	-Non Directive/
	-Supportive/
	-Neutral
		1. Working Alliance
		
		2. Holding Environment
		
		3. Support & Expand
		  A. Self Image
		  B. Ego Functioning
		
		4. Use of
		  A. Transference
		  B. Counter Transference
		  C. Defense Mechanisms
			1. Trusting Relationship
			  Counselor/Client
			2. Safety to Reveal
			  Thoughts, Feelings, Behaviors
			3. Improved
			  A. Sense of Self
			  B. Improved Reality Testing.
			    Impulse Control,
			    Object Relations
			4. Awareness of
			  A. Past Relationships
			    Repeated in Present
			  B. Counselor/Client Dynamics
			  C. Client Defenses
			    vs. trauma & narcissistic injury

SPECIFIC DESIRED RESULTS:
1. Abstinence/Sobriety
2. Understanding Addiction Process
3. Intrapsychic Understanding Translated to Behaviors:
   Self Image; Ego Functioning; Defenses
4. Improved Relationships:
   Family; Work; Friends

(Continued)

44

OVERALL GOAL: TO CHANGE THINKING, FEELING, AND BEHAVIORAL PATTERNS RELATED TO ADDICTION AND PROMOTE DIFFERENTIATION OF INDIVIDUAL AND FAMILY SYSTEM.

THEORETICAL MODEL	COUNSELOR ROLE	MODEL COMPONENTS	MODEL COMPONENTS FOR CHANGE PROMOTE CHANGE THROUGH
2. FAMILY SYSTEMS			
STRUCTURAL Focus: A) Individuals as Part of System B) Present	Directive; Neutral	1. Authority Roles, Decision Making 2. Changing Boundaries (Enmeshed, Fragmented) 3. Shifting Subsystems	1. Changing Role Behaviors & Rules 2. Permeability In & Out of System 3. Shifting From Dependency to Independence, Functionality
STRATEGIC Focus: A) Family/Subsystems B) Present	Directive; Neutral; Catalyst	1. Reframing 2. Paradox 3. Contracts	1. Understanding Maintenance Function of Addiction 2. Destabilizing System 3. Designing Working Plan
BOWEN Focus: A) Individual or Couple B) Present; Past as Relates to Present	Teacher; Coach; Neutral	1. Assessment of 2. (A-E) 2. Cognitive Strategies - Clarifying, Teaching, Coaching to Change A-E A. Differentiation/ A-E Fusion B. Emotional System C. Triangles D. Cutoff E. Family Projection Process	1. & 2 Cognitive Awareness & Understanding to: A. Promote Separation & Differentiation B. Reduce Conflict, Tension C. Realign Relationships D. Deal with Reactive Emotionality E. Take Responsibility for Feelings

SPECIFIC DESIRED RESULTS:
1. Abstinence/Sobriety
2. Understanding Addiction Process
3. Intrapsychic Understanding Translated to Behaviors:
   Self Image; Ego Functioning; Defenses
4. Improved Relationships:
   Family; Work; Friends

1974) and defenses characteristic of borderline and narcissistic personalities often evidenced (i.e., splitting, grandiosity).

It is suggested that the therapeutic relationship of the counselor with the client is key to a favorable outcome. Within the psychodynamic framework the following components are proposed as basic components of the model to be used by the counselor:

1. *Holding Environment.* Holding environment is used here to represent the counseling context, i.e., a safe place for the client to work with the counselor in dealing with thoughts, feelings and behaviors related to the addiction. The therapeutic alliance/relationship is a critical part of this context.

2. *Therapeutic/Working Alliance.* The therapeutic alliance identifies the relationship between the counselor and client that facilitates progress of the client in working through issues. The role of the counselor in promoting the alliance is a function of understanding, empathy and nonjudgmental attitudes (Greenson, 1967).

3. *Transference.* Transference reactions occur when the client experiences the counselor the way (s)he experienced a significant person in the past (usually an early parental figure). The reaction may occur as a positive, negative or erotic transference and is unconscious on the part of the client (Greenson, 1967). Initially a positive transference helps in establishing a therapeutic alliance and may appear as the client being open, expressing good feelings, or idealizing the counselor. In a negative transference the client may exhibit anger or resistance in terms of silence or disagreement. An erotic transference is one in which the client is attracted to the counselor physically or emotionally. This "in love" reaction should be recognized as a transferential reaction based on the wishes and yearnings of past relationships and are not based on a "real" relationship with the counselor. Transference reactions serve as a resistance which may be analyzed, and interpreted with the client whose ego/sense of self is strong enough to handle the stress (usually not until clients are in later stages of recovery). In cases of addicted clients at earlier levels of development exhibiting borderline and narcissistic defenses, the use of the affective expression may be mirrored or reflected in an effort to develop awareness, reality testing and behavioral change.

4. *Defense Mechanisms.* Defense mechanisms are protective re-

sponses to pain or "narcissistic injuries" (Kohut, 1971; Wurmser, 1977; Levin, 1987). Primitive defenses such as denial rationalization, minimization, projection, and splitting are often seen in addicted clients in an effort to deal with anger, rage, depression, etc. The counselor must be able to address the defenses by "respecting" their protective value in defending against pain. In working with the client, Wallace (1989) suggests using the defense mechanisms (preferred defense structure) of the client for his recovery.

5. *Countertransference.* Countertransference is described as the counselor's unconscious reaction to the client (Racker, 1968). This may be the result of the counselor's past experiences or may be a reaction to what the client is communicating. Countertransference can be a useful tool in understanding the client's relationships outside the session and working with the client to change dysfunctional patterns.

Clients who are addicted most frequently present with basic issues of trust and problems in relationships which are related to early psychological development. Commonly seen are issues of loss and abandonment. The psychodynamic framework stresses the relationship between the counselor and client as instrumental in establishing trust and a holding environment safe for the client to surface painful feelings including anger, fear, shame, and depression. It is suggested that by working through feelings and the repetition of behaviors characteristic of early relationships in the transference, that defensive reactions may be addressed and additive behaviors related to impulsiveness, reality testing, and denial may change. Where clients have been stuck in early stages that result in borderline and narcissistic personality disorders characterized by splitting and projection, etc., more work is done with mirroring and/or reflecting feelings in an effort to work on self perception, expanding ego functions and the capacity for establishing object relations. The writer proposes the use of psychodynamics (and information about past history in order to understand the individual in the present), with the counselor taking an active role in supporting ego strengths and building a positive representation of self toward the differentiation of the individual.

In addition to understanding the dynamics of the individual, it is helpful to understand the interactions of the individual in the family. Information related to the interactions is useful in examining the role of addiction as part of the family complementary interactions which support the addiction. The next section describes the use of family systems in addiction counseling.

FAMILY THERAPY

Basic to family systems thinking is the assumption that if the family organization doesn't change the individual will continue to fail and differentiation of the individual and family members will be inhibited. The focus of family therapy is on present behaviors and interactions; the past is used only to understand and change current dysfunctional patterns. Structural, Strategic and Bowen family system theories are described as they relate to addiction.

Structural Family Therapy

Structural Family Therapy (Minuchin, 1981) works with the organizational structure of the family dysfunction as the place of intervention. In chemically addicted families, the addiction is usually accompanied by: dysfunctional parenting, i.e., authority roles between parents and children reversed; enmeshment between a parent (usually the mother) and the addicted child; and disengagement by family members often including the father figure. Alliances and coalitions among subsystems (e.g., parent/child, siblings) serve to support the chemical use.

The role of the counselor is to assess the family vis-à-vis hierarchical roles and sub-systems, decision making, coalitions, boundaries, enmeshment and disengagement all of which determine interaction of systems components in supporting chemical use. Once assessment is made the counselor takes a directive role in changing the organizational structure. The counselor joins the system while remaining separate from it so that (s)he does not become triangulated and ineffective in facilitating change. Changing the structure within the session may be part of shifting roles using the physical space of the counseling context (e.g., parents asked to sit next to each other) for the purpose of moving parents into a united position of authority and begin restructuring appropriate roles for parents and children. This may be an initial attempt at addressing the fusion and/or parentification of children characteristic in chemically addicted families. Empowering parents is accomplished through interventions to shift coalitions and have parent(s) take charge — setting and enforcing rules which may include taking a stand on treatment for the addicted individual, eliminating enabling behaviors (such as giving money to the addict intended for something positive that is used for chemicals), setting curfews and establishing appropriate consequences for inappropriate behaviors. Structural interventions, however, are not exclusive to working with a child as the identified patient in the family.

Adults who have grown up in families characterized by addiction function in their relationships to perpetuate the family dynamics (roles and rules) which they learned growing up. Although chronologically adult, they often continue to manifest dysfunctional behaviors and remain enmeshed with their families. Structural interventions are used in working with adults and family members to change the family structure and help individuals and families separate from each other. The case presented in this paper explains how structural therapy was used to promote differentiation of an addicted male adult who was enmeshed with his family.

Strategic Family Therapy

Strategic therapy (Haley, 1973; Erickson, 1985; Papp, 1983; Madanes, 1981), and family systems theory in general, suggests that addiction is maintained by, and serves to maintain family system interactions.

The role of the therapist in strategic therapy is that of a catalyst in facilitating change between members of the family; contracts may be negotiated with clients. The symptomatic behavior is reframed, i.e., interpreted as being well intentioned but misguided in dealing with the manifested problems, for example, enabling behavior(s) of parent(s) may be interpreted as a manifestation of excessive love in keeping the family together (and thus maintaining the chemical addiction). Paradoxical interventions may also be used in an attempt to reduce resistance to behaviors which have been supporting the addiction. The desired outcome is that family members will see the dysfunctional behavior and be more amenable to change, for example, parent(s) may be encouraged to continue the overzealous caretaking function of the addict by continuing to do everything for him or her (in the service of the family members who are not ready to move on to more independent behaviors or a higher level of differentiation). Strategic techniques include tasks and directives with emphasis on change outside the session, dealing with resistance (going with the resistance) to eliminate power struggles, prescribing symptoms and reframing. The counselor is intensely involved in the intervention and then disengages leaving the family to be responsible for the work outside the session.

Bowen Family Therapy

The goal of Bowen's family systems model (1978) in working with chemical addiction is to facilitate differentiation of individuals by using cognitive and objective approaches in addressing the reactive behaviors characteristic of addicted individuals and family members. A basic assumption is that the system is fused, i.e., there is no clear separation of individual identity, especially between a parent and child; the parent projects anxiety onto the child who then serves as a scapegoat to mask the problem which may include addiction. The counselor usually works with a couple or individual to achieve the goal, the assumption being that changing the interaction of one person will influence interactions with other parts of the system. The counselor takes the role of "coach" or consultant with a focus on thinking and cognitive awareness as opposed to insight, emotional catharsis and supportive techniques. The technique of focusing on cognition is viewed as especially useful in chemically addicted systems characterized by high emotional tension and anxiety. The counselor initially joins with the individual or as part of a triangle with a couple, but remains de-triangulated by remaining objective with a cognitive focus and avoiding transference/countertransference reactions. The model includes assessment of: (1) differentiation of the identified patient and family members with whom work is being done (low differentiation is characteristic of addicted families); (2) the nuclear emotional system, i.e., emotional climate as chaotic, conflicted (addicted families are usually characterized by conflict and anger); (3) triangles which are formed by adding a third member to reduce the emotional tension between two members (in addicted families a common triangle exhibits fusion between one parent and a child while the other parent figure is distanced; one member of the triangle is the addict, often but not exclusively a child); (4) multigenerational process which exhibits addiction and other patterns over two or three generations; and (5) emotional cutoff which occurs when a person attempts to separate from the family, usually triggered by emotional upset (this is often seen by the addict in a pseudo attempt at independence and repeated as the individual leaves and returns home during drinking or drug related crises).

The techniques used in the model include, (1) use of family history in identifying coalitions, intergenerational transmission, fused relationships and cut off patterns; (2) clarification of the relationship between a couple, individual and extended family members; (3) identification of triangular relationships in an attempt to change patterns; (4) use of "I" messages supporting differentiation by taking responsibility for ones thoughts and feelings; (5) ongoing identification, clarification, reassessment and redefinition of goals; (6) assignment of tasks to achieve detriangulation; (7) cognitive focusing and questioning; and (8) coaching strategies (For a detailed description of coaching strategies of engagement, planning, reentry, work, and follow-through, the reader is referred to Carter and McGoldrick, 1976).

PSYCHODYNAMICS AND FAMILY SYSTEMS: CASE APPLICATION

CASE:[2] B. Smith Diagnosis: Alcohol Dependence

B is a recovering white alcoholic male (age 30) who has a drinking history of fifteen years. He admitted to drinking from age 15 with friends (gulping typical of adolescent drinking) and experimenting with marijuana, and LSD. He claims no current use of drugs other than alcohol. B graduated high school and worked at various jobs — delivery boy, cashier, but could not hold a steady job. He married at age 25; after three months his wife left him and he went back home. Since that time, he has worked as a taxi driver, but is not happy with this work. His mother and father are 60 and 65 respectively. B is an only child; his mother had medical problems and could not have any other children. Mrs. Smith does not work; Mr. Smith works part time managing an appliance store. Mr. Smith is assertive, while Mrs. Smith appears passive and depressed. There is a history of alcoholism in the families of both Mr. and Mrs. Smith. B was referred to the outpatient clinic after completing treatment eight months ago. He has been dry, and is attending AA meeting three times a week. He was referred for counseling.

(The counselor used psychodynamics and family systems therapy over a period of two and one-half years. Sessions were held weekly with the client; three sessions with the family during the first three months and two sessions between the sixth and eighth months of treatment.)

PSYCHODYNAMIC ASSESSMENT AND INTERVENTION

The following assessment identifies early developmental problems, transference, countertransference and defensive functioning as related to the problem of addiction and how each was used within the working alliance and holding environment to address addiction. An assessment of B's functioning resulting from individual and family sessions suggests early developmental problems. His mother was hospitalized after B's birth with rheumatic fever and his maternal grandmother took care of him for a period of two weeks; although Mrs. Smith was home, his grandmother continued caring for him primarily for the first two months. Mrs. Smith remained home until B was 3 1/2 and then went to work full time to contribute to the family income. Mr. and Mrs. Smith agree that they spoiled B by giving him everything he asked for. B described his early years as missing his mother and feeling lonely when she was not home for him after school. B did not want to go to school and stayed home with stomachaches frequently through grade five. He maintained average grades (Cs) nevertheless, until he started cutting classes in

9th grade when he recalls starting to drink and smoke pot on weekends with friends; the drinking increased during the week (10th grade) and he started missing school. He would claim to have headaches (possible hangovers) and his mother would make excuses by writing notes for his absence. Mrs. Smith recalls being anxious and always worried that B would not be able to make it through school. She became overprotective toward him. Mr. Smith had little input into B's early and adolescent years as he was working to make ends meet. B wishes he had done more with Mr. Smith like playing ball. B's early and adolescent years are assessed as deficient in obtaining adequate "good enough" parenting related to early absence of his mother and disengagement by his father. His unmet needs inhibited the individuation and separation process necessary in the course of development. His low self esteem and feelings of inadequacy, it is conjectured, are related to these early years when mastery competence identified by Erikson (1959) is built upon early trust development. In an effort to deal with uncomfortable feelings about himself in school he reacted by avoiding (daydreaming, cutting classes, drinking) thereby limiting opportunities for social and cognitive skill development.

In sessions, B would become angry and upset when his dysfunctional behaviors (being late for work, missing work) were addressed. He would deny the relationship of impulsiveness and lack of responsibility in these behaviors to old drinking behaviors. B would project his problems at work on his co-workers and boss and accuse the counselor of not understanding him. He threatened to leave counseling since he "wasn't getting anything out of it." In dealing with the outbursts of anger the counselor was dealing with early *transference reactions* which B experienced when not getting his needs met. *Defensive reactions of denial* of responsibility and *projecting blame* served to cover *feelings of guilt and shame* he had about himself. At times the *counselor would experience frustration and anger* in response to B's anger. *This countertransference* helped the counselor to understand how others experienced B. This information was useful, in working with B to understand the impact of his behavior on others, as a starting point for awareness and taking responsibility for his feelings and slowly changing reactivity to thoughtful responding.

The relationship between B and the counselor simulated early developmental stages of attachment, separation, individuation, and rapprochement (Mahler, 1975). During this period the counselor worked on building a *working alliance* and establishing a *holding environment* as a safe arena to work through anger/rage and feelings of shame. B expressed feeling worthless — not being capable of holding a job, or having skills necessary to be marketable, although he thought he had the ability to do better. As he was able to explore these feelings he recalled feeling depressed and ashamed in school when teachers would call on him and he wouldn't know the answers. He described feeling nauseous when this would happen and would visit the nurse's office frequently. A relationship is suggested between B's parents projecting anxiety about his inability to "make the grade" and his early and later feelings of inadequacy. This *early projection process* had the effect of rendering B feeling incapable and keeping him fused to his mother as he accepted her anxiety as his own. The process was reinforced by his father's non-involvement and similar anxieties about B's capabilities. This admittedly oversimplified explanation (for the purpose of this writing) is offered as a connection to understanding B's feelings of inadequacy on the job and his *defensive functioning* to deal with the feelings of inadequacy. As work on his current functioning and early experiences continued, progress was slowly made in B's efforts to develop new skills. Vocational testing which at first was frightening to him, for it would reinforce his sense of inadequacy, was pursued and he slowly identified abilities which resulted in attending and completing computer school.

Progress was slow but rewarding as the counselor worked with the client over a period of 2 1/2 years. During this time, there were three slips, and B drank. One stress-related slip occurred when his mother was hospitalized and almost died. B's old defensive patterns surfaced, missing work, isolating, missing AA meetings and finally drinking. These behaviors were worked on in sessions as part of the addiction dynamics. Each time the drinking episodes were shorter and it took less time to get back on track. His improved *sense of self, ego functioning* and *awareness of defenses* were instrumental in the process of recovery.

When B first entered counseling he was dating a young woman he met at AA meetings. This relationship terminated when B got jealous of her relationships with other men. He subsequently dated women and repeated a similar pattern. During the sessions his relationship to women was discussed in terms of addiction. B was looking for someone to be there for him who would not let him down. As the sessions progressed B was able to handle the stress of not being symbiotically attached to the relationship (i.e., needing to be with her or in touch with her all the time). He increased attendance at AA and expanded his social networking, both of which were essential in complementing the counseling process. As he was abstinent over a longer period of time his relationships in general and with women in particular were healthier; concomitant with this, the time spent with his mother and calling her decreased. He was able to increasingly talk about his past reactions in cutting off relationships and developing the ability to work through feelings of being threatened and abandoned. At termination he had been in a relationship with a woman for 7 months, the longest period he had maintained. B's defenses of isolation and splitting decreased as his ability to integrate positive and negative feelings related to his girlfriend, boss and co-workers improved.

FAMILY ASSESSMENT AND INTERVENTION

In working with the family, it was evident that B and his mother were symbiotically tied or fused. Using Bowen's model, differentiation (the opposite of fusion) was assessed as low. B spent most of his time with Mrs. Smith, initially living at home after treatment. The nuclear emotional system was characterized by Mrs. Smith's depression, Mr. and Mrs. Smith spending little time together and projected fear by both parents that B would "wind up alcoholic and on the street." The triangular relationship presents a picture of fusion between Mrs. Smith and B, and Mr. Smith in conflict with both (telling Mrs. Smith she was babying B and telling B what he should do with his life). Multigenerational alcoholism was evidenced in Mrs. Smith's family—her father and grandfather. Mrs. Smith described herself as the responsible one in the family (hero child) while her mother dealt with Mrs. Smith's alcoholic father and grandfather. Emotional cutoff was evidenced by B making several attempts to leave the family, the last of which resulted in getting married and then relapsing after their separation and returning home in crisis.

The following family interventions were made by the counselor:

Clarification of Goals (Bowen). The counselor asked each family member to identify what was important for B. Each agreed that abstinence and independence of B was the goal. Mr. and Mrs. Smith were concerned that B was "still" living home with them and had never been on his own. They said they would like to see him married with a family and a responsible job. B also verbalized the desire to be on his own, although he expressed being fearful of doing so. Based on this agreement, the counselor suggested a structural intervention as described.

Structural Intervention. Time was spent working with the family to plan how they might be instrumental in helping move B out and take up residence on his own. This intervention failed, with the family returning and expressing anger at the counselor. They couldn't follow through with the plan and expressed strong sentiment and reasons why B shouldn't move out. B said he felt his parents needed him and he couldn't move out. Underneath the emotion was an issue the Smith family was not ready to deal with, i.e., if B wasn't there, what would happen to their relationship? Their lives focused on worrying about B in school, then with his peers, and over the past fifteen years crises related to his alcohol and drug use.

Strategic Intervention. The counselor shifted gears, admitted making an error (thereby addressing the power struggle with the family) and suggested it was too soon for their plan (as good as it was, and important to all of them) to work. The family needed to be close and live together for a while longer. A prescription for continued living together with Mrs. Smith and B spending most of their time together and Mrs. Smith taking care of B's needs (washing, cooking, etc.) as she had always done.

The result was that over a period of two weeks the Smiths said this arrangement couldn't work—both Mr. and Mrs. Smith were disgusted. B was beginning to feel uncomfortable by his mother's distress. The family suggested they try working toward B's move again. Part of the plan developed with the family included activities for Mrs. Smith including attendance at Al-Anon; Mr. and Mrs. Smith spending time going to dinner or a movie; and Mr. Smith spending time with B discussing his (B's) work. It was also suggested that Mr. Smith share some of the difficulties with B that he had experienced in getting through difficult times in his own work career. The elements in the plan were *activities designed to shift the structure* of the family so that: (1) B could differentiate from the fusion with Mrs. Smith; (2) B could spent time with Mr. Smith discussing problems in dealing with the realities of the work world; (3) Mrs. Smith could get help in letting go of B (detaching) by attending Al-Anon; and (4) ultimately B could leave home more prepared to handle living on his own with less likelihood of returning home in crisis. A time frame was established for B's moving out; the family estimated four months. The actual move took place in six months with B sharing an apartment with an AA buddy. (The move took place one year and four months into treatment.)

Throughout the process the counselor served in the role of teacher/coach as described by Bowen in working to: (1) diffuse the emotional climate; (2) help the family to see intergenerational factors involved in alcohol transmission as a family disease; (3) help family members to identify and change defenses used to support B's drinking, (e.g., enabling defenses of denial regarding absence from school and later from work; rationalization of the need to live at home for B; overprotectiveness serving to maintain the fusion and in turn support the addiction); and (4) clarify plans to help B become independent. Structural and strategic interventions as noted were used with Bowen's components to support the goal of differentiation.

CASE OUTCOME

Termination of counseling occurred when B decided to move to another part of the state where he had been offered a job as a sales clerk in a computer chain. The progress he made can be summarized as increased differentiation evidenced by:

1. Continued working on abstinence and recovery with increasing time periods of abstinence.
2. Improvement in self perception of his work capability, and relationships on the job.
3. More control and less reactivity evidenced by better ego func-

tioning: less impulsive, better reality testing in personal relationships and work-authority relationships.
4. Ability to move out of his parents' home and remain independent, separation from mother, able to identify more with his father.
5. Increasingly able to maintain a relationship with his girlfriend and dealing with feelings of abandonment.
6. More objective thinking in making decisions, improved judgement.
7. Increasing awareness of denial, rationalization, projection (as part of warning signs in slips and relapse) and ability to use coping strategies in dealing with defenses.
8. Increase in attendance at AA which supported all of the foregoing.

Recommendations were made for continued attendance at AA meetings, sponsorship and counseling. The counselor worked in facilitating contacts with referrals in the new location.

CONCLUSION

Differentiation is a goal common to psychodynamic and family systems counseling—psychodynamics focusing on differentiation of the individual, and family systems on the members of the family. In chemical addiction low differentiation is related to addiction with the goal of abstinence, sobriety and recovery a focal point of treatment.

Psychodynamics is presented as a tool to understand the intrapsychic functioning of the client including ego functioning, sense of self, and defensive functioning, each of which is related to early psychological development of the individual. Developing client awareness of the dynamics of addiction related to dysfunctional behaviors such as impulsiveness, poor reality testing, defensive functioning and relationship problems is part of the counseling process. Psychodynamically the counselor works with transference, countertransference and defense mechanisms as they relate to the addiction.

Problems are worked out through the working alliance between the counselor and client, and translation to the client's relationships in everyday life may be expected in terms of better ego functioning, stronger sense of self, better relationships and overall differentiation. Abstinence from chemicals as evidenced by the client is supported and related to psychodynamic functioning as the client progresses in the recovery process.

Family systems focuses on the interactions between family members in an effort to change codependency patterns and facilitate differentiation. Complementary interactions (codependency) of members support the continuation of addiction. Family systems interventions as proposed are directed to: (1) changing the organization of the system by changing roles and coalitions supporting the addiction (Structural Therapy); (2) working with the addiction and supporting interactions to change the maintenance of addiction by prescriptions which destabilize the system (Strategic Therapy); and (3) using a cognitive approach to diffuse the emotionality of the addicted system thereby promoting differentiation of individual members and, in turn, the system (Bowen Therapy).

The writer suggests the use of psychodynamics and family systems as an integrated and complementary approach in enhancing the potential of individual and family systemic change in working with chemical addiction.

NOTES

1. Chemical addiction is used to include addiction to alcohol and other drugs.
2. Case material has been changed as necessary to protect anonymity of client.

REFERENCES

Bean, M. & Zinberg, N. (Eds.). (1981). *Dynamic approaches to the understanding and treatment of alcoholism*. New York: Macmillan Press, Inc.
Bowen, M. (1978). *Family therapy in clinical practice*. New York: Jason Aronson.
_____. (1976). In Guerin, R. *Family therapy: Theory and practice*. (pp. 42-90). New York: Gardner Press.
Bradshaw, J. (1988). *Bradshaw on the family: A revolutionary way of self-discovery*. Deerfield Beach, FL: Health Communications, Inc.
Campbell, R.J. (1981). *Psychiatric dictionary*. 5th Ed. New York: Oxford University Press, Inc.

Carter, E. & McGoldrick Orfandis, M. (1976). In Guerin, P. *Family therapy and practice*. (pp. 193-219). New York: Gardner Press.

Erickson, M. (1985). In Zeig, J. ed. *Ericksonian psychotherapy*. Vol. 2. New York: Brunner Mazel.

Greenson, R.R. (1967). *The Technique and Practice of Psychoanalysis* (pp. 151-216). New York: International University Press, Inc.

Guerin, P.J. (Ed.), (1976). *Family Therapy Theory and Practice*. New York: Gardner Press, Inc.

Haley, J. (1973). *Uncommon Therapy*. New York: W.W. Norton & Co., Inc.

Haley, J. (Ed.), (1985). *Conversations with Milton Erikson, M.D.* Vol. 3, New York: W.W. Norton & Co., Inc.

Khantzian, E. (1977). The ego, the self, and opiate addiction: theoretical and treatment considerations. In Blaine, J. and Julius, D. *Psychodynamics of Drug Dependence*. NIDA Research Monograph 12. Washington, D.C.: U.S. Department of Health, Education & Welfare.

Kaufman, E. (1985). Family systems and family therapy of substance abuse: An overview of two decades of research and clinical experience. *International Journal of the Addictions*. 20(6 & 7):897-916.

Kohut, H. (1971). *The Analysis of the Self. New York: International University Press*.

Levin, J.D. (1987). *Treatment of Alcoholism and Other Addictions. A Self Psychology Approach*. New Jersey: Jason Aronson, Inc.

Levin, J.D. (1990). *Alcoholism: A Biopsychosocial Approach*. New York: Hemisphere Publishing Corporation.

Madanes, C. (1981). *Strategic Family Therapy*. San Francisco, CA: Jossey-Bass Publishers.

Minuchin, S., & Fishman, H.C. (1981). *Family Therapy Techniques*. Cambridge, MA: Harvard University Press.

· Papp, P. (1983). *The Process of Change*. New York: Guilford Press.

Racker, H. (1968). *Transference and Countertransference*. New York: International University Press.

Wallace, J. (1989). *John Wallace: Writings*. Newport, RI: Edgehill Publications.

Wegscheider, S. (1981). *Another Chance*. Palo Alto, CA: Science and Behavior Books, Inc.

Wurmser, L. (1974). Psychoanalytic considerations of the etiology of compulsive drug use. *Journal of the American Psychoanalytic Association*, 22:820-843.

———. (1977). In Blaine, J. and Julius, D. *Psychodynamics of Drug Dependence*. NIDA Research Monograph 12. Washington, D.C., U.S. Department of Health, Education and Welfare.

Zimberg, S., Wallace, J., & Blume, S. ((Eds.). (1985). *Practical Approaches to Alcoholism Psychotherapy*. New York: Plenum Publishing Corporation.

Planned Family Intervention: Johnson Institute Method

Ellen Faber, MA, CAC
Beverly Keating-O'Connor, MA, CAC

SUMMARY. This paper outlines the process of Planned Family Intervention, Johnson Institute Method. The authors explain that, although too seldom used, Planned Family Intervention is an extremely successful and appropriate response to the disease of chemical dependency. They describe five widely held myths which hinder family and friends, and many family therapists, from offering help to the chemically dependent person. They also present the major educational themes and the dynamics which lead to a well-orchestrated and successful intervention. Planned Intervention is presented as a beginning of family recovery for this family disease.

A FAMILY RESPONSE TO A FAMILY DISEASE

The planned Family Intervention Process was pioneered by Vernon Johnson in Minnesota in the early 1970s. He carefully outlined the method in *I'll Quit Tomorrow* (1980). Dr. Johnson observed how some employers confronted dysfunctional employees about their poor performance with tough love: giving them the choice of treatment or a consequence regarding the person's job — *a bottom line*. He realized that groups of "significant others" had the same ability to take a tough stand with the addict. The purpose of such an Intervention is: (1) to present the facts of the Chemically

Ellen Faber is a therapist specializing in Planned Family Intervention and treatment of chemically dependent families. She is Director of Intervention Associates in Belle Mead, NJ. Her book, *Handbook for Intervention*, will be published this Spring. Beverly Keating-O'Connor is a therapist who has conducted Planned Family Interventions for the past five years while supervising the Outpatient Addiction Treatment Services at the Medical Center at Princeton in Princeton, NJ.

Dependent Person's (CDP) use of substances in a non-judgmental way that will pierce the CDP's defenses and denial (2) to offer immediate help, that day, to the affected person, and (3) to assist the family in taking a stand to care for themselves and initiate their own recovery *regardless* of what the CDP chooses to do (Picard, 1989).

Dr. Johnson formulated a "tough love" process patterned after the corporate interventions he observed. This was later outlined in *Intervention* (1986). This tough approach was designed for a *cohesive group of friends and family members* to take a *stand* with the alcoholic and present the *specific facts* of the drinking in a *loving and caring way* coupled with an offer of *immediate help*. If treatment is refused, the team members take *a stand* in the form of bottom lines regarding how they will proceed to take care of themselves. The family members' formulation of bottom lines, though often unstated in the actual intervention, is extremely important.

There is much misunderstanding about both the disease of Chemical Dependency and Planned Intervention (Picard, 1989). Dr. Johnson's initial interventions (*I'll Quit Tomorrow*, 1980) were often confrontive, angry and placating to the CDP. The process of Intervention has been refined in the past ten years, eliminating argument and refining the process to disallow the CDP's choosing his own treatment. In the past decade, it has become apparent there is a need for more in-depth family education and preparation.

THE MAJOR MYTHS

Five major myths are widely held by family, friends, and professional therapists. These myths discourage individuals from altering the course of addiction by doing a Planned Intervention (Spickard and Thompson, 1985).

Myth #1. The CDP must want help before he/she can get it. Wrong. CDPs are in denial. They say, "I choose to drink; it's not a problem." The process of Intervention is designed to pierce the CDP's defense system and denial, so that he/she will briefly be in touch with the inner pain of addiction, and accept immediate help (Morgan and Silver, 1980).

Myth #2. The CDP must hit bottom before he/she gets help.

Death is bottom for the CDP. Waiting for the bottom, therefore, or waiting for a spontaneous awakening on the part of the CDP can be dangerous. Instead, intervention creates a bottom, and an opportunity for the CDP to get professional help.

Myth #3. The CDP will quit drinking or using drugs on his/her own. Almost every co-dependent is hoping and waiting for the day when the CDP will realize his/her problem and stop drinking or using drugs for good. They have heard of this happening to others. Also, the CDP may have quit before, proving to the family that he/she can if he/she wants to. Unfortunately, most CDPs will continue to drink or use drugs, and die of addiction, unless there is some type of intervention.

Myth #4. No one has the right to interfere with another's life. When the CDP's drinking or drug use is affecting the well-being of others they do have a right to address that issue and take a stand about it. Also, this myth assumes that the CDP is doing what he/she is doing by choice. Actually, the disease of chemical dependency removes the element of choice about the use of chemicals. Once an addiction has taken hold, it becomes a physiological imperative to continue drinking or using drugs (Spickard and Thompson, 1985).

Myth #5. Intervention might make the situation worse. Family members often ask "What if he never speaks to me again afterward?" Again, by hesitating to address a fatal illness, codependents become enablers and the alcoholic may reject or abuse people close to them even if they don't intervene. Others fear that the CDP will commit suicide. The fact is, the CDP is already slowly committing suicide through the use of chemicals and is taking the family down as well. (These authors and Johnson Institute have had no experience of suicide after a carefully planned Family Intervention.)

THE NEED FOR A PROFESSIONAL INTERVENTIONIST

Planned Intervention is an intricate process requiring a counselor who is (1) knowledgeable about all aspects of alcohol and drug addiction, (2) familiar with the concept of the illness as a family disease, (3) specifically trained in Intervention techniques, (4) experienced in doing Interventions, (5) an educator and a good teacher about addiction and Intervention, (6) a supportive and insightful therapist for the family team during this emotional process, and (7) knowledgeable about treatment resources. Doctors, therapists, and other health professionals need to be aware of when it is appropriate to refer a codependent to an Intervention Specialist for an evaluation (Picard, 1989). An important role of the intérventionist is assisting in the selection of team members (Krupnick and Krupnick, 1985; Meagher, 1987). Only caring individuals should be included. Candidates used are immediate family members, relatives, neighbors, doctors, clergymen, and lawyers (Spickard and Thompson, 1985).

This process should not be attempted by counselors who do not meet the above criteria and who are not thoroughly trained in this process *and* who have *not* dealt with any personal material which is reactivated by the Intervention process. This material usually has its roots in their own dysfunctional family situation which may not have been resolved for the therapist (Bratton, 1987).

INTERVENTION AND AL-ANON

It has been written that the Intervention is the opposite of the detachment that Al-Anon suggests (Hawthorne, 1985). It is our belief that detachment is appropriate *after* specific professional help has been offered to get the CDP into treatment. Chemical Dependency is a progressive illness which is 100 percent fatal if left untreated. Death can occur from severe disruption of organ functions, a general breakdown in the body's immune system, accidents or suicide. The progressive nature of addiction has been described by many authors (Johnson, 1980; Wegscheider, 1981). When faced with such severe consequences, to detach and turn our backs is highly inappropriate *if* we have not done all we can to offer treatment (Pinkham, M., 1986).

INTERVENTION BREAKS FAMILY RULES

The process of preparing a planned Intervention flies in the face of three rigid CDP family rules. These rules have held the addiction in place and prevented recovery. They are:

1. *Don't talk*: In the Intervention process, participants are encouraged to share specific information with each other about the CDP's drinking or drug use. Often family members will report feelings of betrayal. They are breaking the unspoken family rule *not* to talk about the drinking or drug use.

2. *Don't feel*: In an Intervention, families are offered encouragement and support for getting in touch with their feelings. This is often difficult since most codependents have suppressed feelings in order to survive.

3. *Don't trust*: Persons from chemically dependent families do not trust. Often they do not trust themselves or their own reactions. And they don't trust other people, especially outsiders such as therapists who "don't know our situation." The fact that a family presents for Intervention indicates that they are desperate and are hurting enough to begin to trust outside help (Caldwell, 1986; Ketcham and Gustafson, 1989).

The Intervention counselor must provide a safe and supportive atmosphere for families to risk talking and feeling.

MAJOR DYNAMICS OF INTERVENTION

There are three essential components to a Planned Family Intervention:

1. A cohesive group of significant others who agree that the drinking or drug use is a problem and agree that the Intervention is the appropriate method to get the CDP into treatment. Obviously, in many chemically dependent families, there will be dissention. Those who do not agree with the method or do not get along in the group will either self-select out of the group, or be asked not to participate. It is important that team members support each other in forming a united front (Maxwell, 1977).

2. Specific facts are presented in a loving, caring and non-judgmental way, using words that the CDP can hear as non-threatening. There are no threats in an Intervention. Team members speak in declarative sentences, often starting with "I." "I saw this happen and felt sad" (Wegscheider, S., 1981).

3. Immediate help is presented to the CDP. Often family members and friends have told the CDP previously to do something

about their drinking or drug use. Sometimes the CDP will agree about the need to "do something," but because the concept is vague, nothing is usually done. Planned Family Intervention always includes the offer of immediate professional help *that day*. The suitcase is packed and ready to go. The appropriate treatment center has been researched and chosen by the family members or team leader. A bed has been reserved or an initial session scheduled by the family for the day of the Intervention. The offer of treatment is immediate in order to capitalize on the temporary vulnerability of the CDP. He or she has just been confronted with powerful, emotional descriptions of his or her behavior and its consequences, from all or most of those individuals who are significant in the life of the CDP. It is in this brief post-intervention period that the CDP, seeing the united front of all those who care, and hearing the evidence of the disease, will accept professional help (Maxwell, 1977). Most often, the CDP's reaction is "They can't all be wrong" and "I didn't realize I was hurting you so much."

THE EDUCATIONAL COMPONENT

Family members and significant others receive thorough education about addiction and the Intervention process from a trained Intervention counselor (Caldwell, 1986). The education explains the disease concept, the primary nature of chemical dependency, denial, enabling, and how to communicate feelings. This education empowers the family who has previously held misconceptions about the disease. As the family refocuses their anger on the *disease* as the culprit and not the CDP, they began to feel more powerful (Bratten, 1987). Family members are also coached in the creation of a bottom line and the communications of feelings by using new and perhaps unfamiliar feeling words. The educational components are summarized below:

1. *Primary Disease*: Chemical Dependency is a primary disease (Mann, 1972). Addressing the chemical dependency first is the entry-way into recovery. It is the first problem which must be addressed, even though there may be a myriad of other psycho-social problems. Any attempts to deal with these related problems will be unsuccessful until the actual chemical dependency is addressed. All

psycho-social problems are contaminated by the problems associated with the addiction (see Figure 1).

2. *Denial*: Family denial is called "The Conspiracy of Silence" (Knowlton and Chaitin, 1990). The family denial weakens during the Intervention process. It is explained that the CDP, still in denial ("I don't have a problem"), needs an Intervention in order to get help to break through that denial (Ketcham and Gustafson, 1989; Morgan and Silver, 1980). It is the loving tone, coupled with specific incidents of drinking which disarms the CDP's defenses (see Figure 2).

3. *Enabling*: The nature of enabling and over-responsible behavior are outlined to the Intervention team. It is explained that family and friends, and often well-meaning professionals, form an enabling system which unwittingly holds the addiction in place and keeps the CDP from feeling the consequences of his actions. The major components of enabling are minimizing and rescuing behaviors (Drews, 1980; Maxwell, 1986).

4. *Recovery for Family and CDP*: The treatment goal for the

FIGURE 1

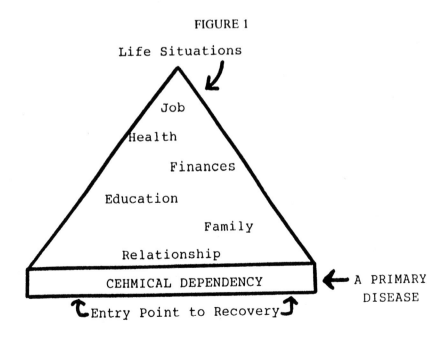

FIGURE 2. Alcoholic Defense System

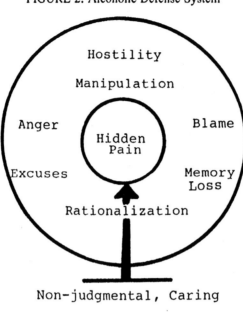

CDP is to comply with the Intervention team's offer of immediate treatment. Recovery for family members means continuing in an educational and 12-step program in order to break the codependent addiction to the CDP. Intervention often frees the family to place their own recovery as a first priority. Some consider it a mistake to even agree to work toward intervention with a family unless they agree to make a firm commitment to continuing recovery for themselves (Bratton, 1987).

5. *Communication of Feelings and Specific Data about the Addiction*: The intervention is based on the ability to break through their own euphoric recall and denial in order to present specific incidents about the drinking or drug use as well as feelings of sadness, fear, abandonment, disappointment, helplessness, and powerlessness. Although feelings of anger are quite normal, its expression is absolutely discouraged because it is inconsistent with the loving and caring tone of the Intervention. It is this tone of love

which disarms the defenses of the CDP. The Intervention counselor will coach each member of the team to use words which convey caring. The counselor will also assist the spouse or other close persons to formulate a personal stand, or bottom line, which forms the structural basis of an Intervention.

THE BOTTOM LINE

Planned Intervention is a structured and powerful response to chemical dependency. The entire process rests firmly on the key person's stand or bottom line. (As previously stated, the actual verbalizing of the bottom lines to the CDP is usually unnecessary since the majority of CDPs readily agree to treatment.) The bottom line is a firm stand regarding what the key person (usually the spouse) and other team members will do *if the CDP refuses treatment*. It is the answer to questions such as: "If your CDP refuses to accept the help you are offering, where does that leave you? How will you take care of yourself (and perhaps children) and continue your own recovery from co-dependency?" (Knowlton and Chaitin, 1990).

The Intervention is perceived as opening the family system to new ways for family members to behave. It is the *beginning* of a family recovery process, and the cornerstone of that recovery is the stated stand, a variation of "I can't live this way anymore – this is what I need to do to take care of myself." A boss may request termination; a spouse may want to live separately; children may set boundaries around drinking behavior and state their intention to continue getting help (Lizotte, 1987).

The Intervention is generally as strong as the resolve of the significant others to hold firmly to their bottom lines. It is emphasized that these bottom lines are not a punishment to the CDP, but a way of becoming responsible to one's self. The Intervention counselor must be supportive during this process of choosing a bottom line.

CONCLUSION

Planned Family Intervention is a structured process which dramatically opens a previously closed family system. Participants are educated about addiction and coached in communicating caring words, stating personal needs and feelings, and in implementing behavior changes (Drews, 1980). These behavior changes by the codependents stop the enabling behavior and take the codependent from being part of the problem to being part of the solution. Inpatient codependency treatment programs are often suggested for the family members, as well as on-going outpatient follow-up and involvement in a 12 step program.

Planned Family Intervention is a process which, when used effectively by trained interventionists, always has a positive outcome whether the CDP goes to treatment or not. If the intervention process is skillfully conducted, the family will become aware of new behaviors and communication skills, and new ways of interacting within the family (Calwell, 1986). The "don't talk" rule has been broken. All involved have begun to look at themselves and the effects the CDP's behavior has had on them, and they realize the part they played in enabling the addiction to go on. The CDP has been exposed; the truth is out, and he or she will never be able to drink or use drugs in the same way again. All the significant persons in the CDP's life have witnessed the truth from everyone else. Unless the CDP is one of those rare individuals described by Alcoholics Anonymous who is "constitutionally incapable of getting honest," his or her use of alcohol/drugs will be affected to a degree which will eventually result in the CDP's seeking treatment.

It is the experience of interventionists that there is nothing to lose, and much to be gained, in using this Intervention Process. It is a powerful and effective tool to be used to improve the lives of those suffering from chemical dependency. Hopefully, as the knowledge of its effectiveness becomes more widespread in the treatment community, more and more professionals will obtain the necessary training to use the Planned Family Intervention method to transform the lives of those affected by the disease of chemical dependency.

REFERENCES

Bratten, M. (1987). *A guide to family intervention*. Florida: Health Communications, Inc.

Bratten, M. (1987). "From denial and delusion to reality and recovery: A family therapist's guide to the intervention process," *Focus on Chemically Dependent Families*. 10(4), 24-25.

Caldwell, J. (1986). "Preparing a family for intervention," *Journal of Psychoactive Drugs*, 18(1), 57-59.

Drews, T. (1980). *Getting Them Sober*. New Jersey: Bridge Publishing.

Hawthorne, W. (1985). "Al-anon and family intervention: Resolving conflicts in philosophy," *Focus on Family and Chemical Dependency*, 8(6), 31, 34-35, 41.

Johnson, V. (1980). *I'll quit tomorrow*. New York: Harper and Row.

Johnson, V. (1986). *Intervention: How to help someone who doesn't want help*. Minneapolis: Johnson Institute.

Ketcham, K. & Gustafson, G. (1989). *Living on the edge: A guide to intervention for families with drug and alcohol problems*. New York: Bantam Books.

Knowlton, J. and Chaitin, B. (1990). *Detachment*. Minnesota: Hazeldon.

Knowlton, J., & Chatin, B. (1990). *Enabling*. Minnesota: Hazeldon.

Krupnick L., & Krupnick, E. (1985). *From despair to Decision*. Minneapolis: Compcare.

Lizotte, K. (1987). "Monday morning seven A.M.: A first-hand look at family intervention," *Focus on Chemically Dependent Families*, 10(2), 12-13, 17-18.

Mann, M. (1972). *Marty Mann's new primer on alcoholism*. New York: Holt, Rinehart, and Winston.

Maxwell, R. (1986). *Beyond the booze battle*. New York: Random House.

Maxwell, R. (1977). *The booze battle*. New York: Ballantine.

Meagher, M. D. (1987). *Beginning of a miracle*. Pompano Beach: Health Communications, Inc.

Morgan, R. and Silver R. (1980). "Counselor's casebook: Enabling — How do you help someone with a drinking problem who doesn't want help?" *Alcoholism*, 1(2), 48-49.

Picard, F. (1989). *Family Intervention*. Oregon: Beyond Words Pub., Inc.

Pinkham, M. (1986). *How to stop the one you love from drinking*. New York: Putnam.

Spickard, A., & Thompson, B. (1985). *Dying for a drink*. Texas: Word Books.

Wegscheider, S. (1981). *Another chance: Hope and health for the alcoholic family*. California: Science and Behavior Books, Inc.

Neuro-Linguistic Programming as Psychotherapeutic Treatment in Working with Alcohol and Other Drug Addicted Families

Chelly M. Sterman, ACSW, BCD, CAC

SUMMARY. The focus of Neuro-Linguistic Programming is, from a psychotherapeutic perspective, on the various change processes that enable individuals and families to function with an increased repertoire of coping choices. NLP validates existing individual and interpersonal belief systems but seeks to expand these to accommodate more appropriate and useful ones based on implementing and building internal and relationship resources. This chapter presents an overview of NLP concepts and techniques relevant to families in addiction recovery. This includes reframing, use of representational systems particularly in calibration, development of rapport and congruent treatment strategies, anchoring techniques, and the trauma and phobia fixes.

INTRODUCTION

A bright, educated couple, married for sixteen years, parents of both an eight year old and a five year old girl, recently entered therapy. The husband and wife were deeply involved in NA as well as AA attendance, the man being sober eight months, the woman six months. Both partners were committed to the relationship and the family—they were earnest, but had felt unsuccessful in their previous involvement in therapy. The woman accused the husband

Chelly M. Sterman is President of Chelly Sterman Associates in Hightstown, NJ. She is a private practitioner and lectures at Rutgers University. Correspondence may be sent to the author at 441 Route 130, Hightstown, NJ 08520.

73

of "letting me down, never being there for me," while he dreaded his wife's "anger and control" issues.

Striking about this couple was the incongruency between their adult verbal relations and the childlike voices, postures and attitudes.

Upon closer examination, the man felt approximately ten years old during the couple's communications, the woman about fourteen. When the man was ten, he was blamed consistently for his parents' marital discord as well as the mother's alcoholism — the marriage ended in divorce shortly thereafter. When the woman was fourteen, her mother had just died from a fall while under the influence of alcohol, an event that the woman blamed on her harsh and unfeeling alcoholic father. This experience created total chaos and a sense of unreality in her life. For some time, the focus was on the partners' attempt in the present to hold down adult roles in a complicated family system in recovery while feeling like desperate children who had failed in their family of origin. Presented with this reframe, the partners felt validated and began to free up resources essential for creating movement in therapy (Bandler, 1985). Though remaining cautious and hyper-vigilant, the couple experienced hope through the understanding and experience that individuals grow from children to adults by installing the appropriate resources. This made it sufficiently safe for each partner to set personal boundaries and respect the other's individual parameters, a required step towards health in addicted families.

NLP: PRIMARY FOCUS AND CONCEPTS

The above case demonstration exemplifies some specific NLP presuppositions and strategies. This chapter does not allow for a broader scope of the basic components of Neuro-Linguistic Programming and I refer to the literature for specific information about NLP components such as linguistic and eye-patterns (Dilts, 1983), the metamodel (Cameron, 1985, Grinder and Bandler, 1976), sorting mechanisms and belief systems (Dilts, 1983), basic human programs (Cameron and Lebeau, 1985) and the use of submodalities in introducing rapid change (Bandler, 1985, Andreas, 1987). Some of this information, however, will be incorporated in this chapter.

The Parts

NLP postulates, along with other therapeutic conceptual frameworks, that individuals contain "inner children," those parts of self that do not progress beyond traumatic childhood experiences. Under certain circumstances, which form triggers or anchors, these "inner child" parts are activated, may actually largely take over from the "adult" which, in taxing situations creates a deficiency of adult resources, both on an internal as well as interpersonal level. These individuals then have perceptual frameworks which are incongruent with adult roles in society at large, especially noticeable within their families, where old triggers have the greatest opportunity of being elicited. The unconscious mind will repeat, as though frozen in time, behaviors that may not be functional in the present, but were the saving grace for that individual at the time of the dreaded life event. In the case of the aforementioned couple, by remaining a ten year old, the man continued to "prove" to his parents that he was not to blame, while the woman, as a fourteen year old, expressed her anger at her father over the death of her mother while maintaining control over her life. Prior to sobriety, of course, the couple's addiction had facilitated those triggered childhood stages over and over again. In other words, the addiction had become, in a paradoxical sense, the couple's primary resource in dealing with unresolved childhood trauma. In early recovery, the addiction as "resource" had been eliminated, leaving the couple feeling fearful and, again paradoxically, almost more like failures then during their active addition.

Neuro-Linguistic Programming places primary importance on the tenet that the therapist needs to validate the intent of the clients' behavior and shift the focus of the behavior to this intent rather that its behavioral manifestation. In regard to this couple, this meant. demonstrating that even though the behavior (his withdrawal, her anger and control) did not work any longer in their present family system, the intent in their respective childhoods was valid, since each designed specific ways, at the time age appropriate, by which they protected themselves most competently in a threatening environment.

NLP—Therapy as a Process

A second NLP tenet comes into play here as well: given the opportunity, the human organism automatically moves towards well being. Its corollary is: the intent of therapy is to add choices to individuals' internal repertoires, and never to take choices away—emotionally costly choices are automatically used less and less as more functional choices are added to the clients' model of the world. Energy then becomes directed toward an inviting, a compelling, future and momentum towards well being becomes stronger as internal resources are accessed and become available. In the above example, when the couple began to perceive their dysfunctional behavior as a childhood resource, rather than only as an internal and external struggle in the present, each became capable of modulating the behavior. NLP focuses extensively on this reframing process and presents specific models for reframing techniques such as the six-step reframe (Bandler and Grinder, 1979) and the negotiation model (Bandler and Grinder, 1982).

Focus on Results

A third tenet of NLP is that individuals generally have all the internal resources they need to lead competent and successful lives, and that in the process of living people lose access to these resources by focusing on necessary survival mechanisms. When therapy is organized as though this is true, the outcomes achieved appear to have a greater chance of being successful. The reason for this, according to NLP, is that the focus is on a future of well being, a process, rather than on a present immobilized problem state. In the case described above, the partners each had a repertoire of resources—both were professionals, had many friends and were accomplished in a variety of areas. What they had lost, however, or had not further developed as a result of their traumatic life events, was access to a repertoire of behavioral choices each time an old trigger state indicating potential danger to the individual in a childhood or early adolescent state became activated within the family context. Childhood events preempted functional behavior in the present marital relationship each time anchors such as fear, (loss of) control, abandonment, humiliation, etc. were touched, a frequent occurrence in every recovering family system. Traumatic childhood stages take on a frozen quality and NLP frequently focuses on dislodging these stuck states and creating a flow toward the present or future.

Rapport Skills

In the initial stages of therapy, NLP distinguishes a process called "pacing," which signifies the therapist's task of joining clients in their model of the world to create an alliance between the client, the family system and the "leading." By pacing, the family receives assurance that the changes to be introduced are what NLP calls "ecological," congruent with, fitting in the family's model of reality. It is essential to "pace" in the psychotherapeutic relationship, to join the clientsystem's model of the world before "leading," inviting that clientsystem to participate in a change process. During this stage, NLP places much emphasis on the clients' representational systems by careful calibration of visual, auditory, and kinesthetic clues which are expressed in eye patterns, voice tones, postures, skin coloration, etc. In addition to the clients' verbalizations, these systematic calibrations provide a wealth of reliable information to the therapist, especially during the formation stage of the relationship with the clientsystem. NLP emphasizes the appropriateness of a shift through therapeutic intervention in the family system. This ecology involves a process NLP calls future-pacing, a process whereby a desired result is connected, as the term indicates, to various elements of the future of the individual and family to assure the appropriateness of the outcomes established in therapy for the family system.

BASIC HUMAN PROGRAMS

Reframing frozen scenes to include age appropriate distinctions is an essential component of the family healing process. Robert Dilts (1983), one of the early and most prolific contributors to Neuro-Linguistic Programming writing, distinguished three internal and family states that create "stuck states" or static problem states. The first one, helplessness, is a condition where goals are perceived as possible, but the family does not view itself as capable of achieving them. In the second one, hopelessness, goals are experienced as not achievable, regardless of the family's capabilities. In the third state, worthlessness, the family labors under the belief that as individuals and as a family as a whole specific goals are not deserved, which connects to shame issues, a focus of much of the present writing on addiction. Dilts describes this concept as a set of basic beliefs which connect the family to an immobilized state as well as Connirae and Steve Andreas (1987). These authors also describe the skills required for constructing congruent belief systems and basic human programs, and they demonstrate how to enrich the ways individual clients and families can "sort" for their perceptual realities. To reiterate, moving beyond symptom removal, as described above, NLP techniques focus on the individual's and family's internal and interpersonal perception of reality and promote changes which modify the beliefs and perceptions which shape and limit the family system.

FAMILY TASKS IN RECOVERY

In recovering families, several tasks present themselves to individuals as well as the family system. In the first place, the family needs to grieve for its losses and, in most families, there are many losses on a variety of levels. Some grieving will be congruent for family members, but most grieving occurs on an individual level and needs to be paced carefully by the therapist as well as by other family members. It is a great contribution to the family system when, for instance, one parent can support the anger/anxiety phase of the grieving process in a child and a husband can create an accepting atmosphere for his spouse's depression. It is often the first time that family members can (a) contribute to each other and (b) be validated by one another. Issues of selfworth and mutual respect often get their first chance at expression in this phase when parents and children begin to feel effective in the family by utilizing the pacing and leading processes.

NLP perceives the therapist often as a translator of behaviors, thoughts, feeling, emotions and motivations between family members, observing the need for pacing, reframing and the ecology of the process as the clientsystem begins to move away from the addictions and concomitant trauma and pain and towards the tasks at hand. This next process, according to Davis (expected publication date: 1990), involving specific interpersonal tasks, is a more focused problem solving state which requires the development of improved individual and interactional communication skills. In this state key strategies which are preferential to those established originally by the use of alcohol and other drugs in the family system can effectively be created. One primary task here is the move toward intimacy which, prior to sobriety, is often largely regulated by the drug of abuse and its place in the family system.

Accessing Resources

The elimination of drinking and drug related behavior remaining central, NLP focuses family members on the task of finding alternative behaviors that correspond with key family functions. The family is assisted in discovering and accessing resources that will make the function of the addictive substance obsolete. Neuro-Linguistic Programming provides a variety of skills and strategies to reconnect family members to themselves and each other on both conscious and unconscious levels and to create effective and efficient models for working on and accomplishing interpersonal tasks (Davis, expected publication date: 1990). Given that the addicted member of the family is accustomed to immediate relief for discomfort as well as the phenomenon of a high state of anxiety in early sobriety and abstinence among family members, an additional advantage of using NLP skills and strategies is the opportunity to create rapid, measurable, observable change. A component of this rapid success is the emphasis on rapport between the therapist and the client system and, as part of this, the use of reframing, a consistent validation of the clients in areas where, prior to treatment, they were customarily blamed by others or themselves.

Resource States

NLP enables therapists to create rapid changes in individuals and families by using such specific techniques as the six-step reframe (Bandler and Grinder, 1979), the trauma and phobia fixes (Bandler,

1985, Bandler and Grinder, 1979), swish patterns, and behavior generators (Bandler, 1985). Neuro-Linguistic Programming, through these techniques, installs or creates access to resourceful states which allow family members a broader response base in dealing with family issues. These sometimes dramatic changes become solid building blocks for ongoing self directed changes. As stated before, the family automatically moves towards well being, since the unconscious minds of individuals move in the direction of the least resistance. This principle, used consciously in NLP techniques, sets the stage for increasingly less dependent and more autonomous behavior for the alcoholic or otherwise drug-dependent individual and his family. The speed with which changes occur reduces the addicted person's need for external reward seeking behavior and reduces the anxiety of the family members, which again becomes a resource in the family's move towards increased health. A sense of hope is reestablished, families feel less helpless, and they begin to rebuild their sense of worth and self-respect.

Anchoring Techniques

An important contribution of NLP to substance abuse treatment is the conscious use of anchoring techniques. The presence of alcohol and other drug related behavior in a recovering family can trigger a whole set of previously learned interpersonal responses in a family system that in many respects may be solidly on its way to recovery. As demonstrated in the first case example, this elicits behavior from an earlier, anxiety ridden, dreaded family state which may threaten the newly conquered, but yet fragile, family sobriety or abstinence. Neuro-Linguistic Programming, in a reframe technique partially borrowed from Ericsonian hypnotherapy, emphatically teaches the family to perceive all information as feedback, rather than failure, information about what the family needs to formulate, learn next, experiment with, and test out. The important issue here is to add choices to the family's repertoire of feelings and behavior rather than narrowing it down by determining particular behaviors or outcomes as failure. All emotions, thoughts and actions which the family reports are a form of feedback, even if it does not correspond to the initial goal, the desired state. What could be termed failure then merely becomes a place to reevaluate what the next step in the therapeutic process needs to be.

Relapses, interruptions in sobriety and abstinence, are treated in this fashion as well, maintaining the state of hope, independence and selfworth essential for a family involved in a healing process, in its movement towards well being, and on its way to a compelling future. A concomitant advantage is that if shame and guilt are not introduced as part of the "slip," it is generally easier for the substance abuser to terminate the relapse, and terminate earlier in this relapse process. Since little attention is paid to the negative connotation of the relapse by the use of the reframe, the family as a whole uses less emotional energy on a "slip," is less depleted as a result and is more capable of retaining newly won advances in the creation of a healthy family system.

INCREASING LIFE CHOICES

Essential in the NLP repertoire is the creation of alternative feelings and behaviors which become as automatic as the drinking and drug using behavior was prior to sobriety and abstinence. Congruent with this concept, much attention is paid to testing the installed behaviors to check that any change has become actually the property of the family allowing the family's conscious attention to be focused on presenting family tasks. It is important that old triggers, a look or tone of a parent or spouse, a particular posture of the child, become detached from previously established responses, which had followed a conditioned pattern. When one family member becomes capable of choosing new behaviors under old circumstances, the whole family becomes compelled to create new participatory behaviors, creating choice on two levels: in the first place there is the possibility of establishing more productive behaviors, and secondly, initially even more importantly, and more reliably, the opportunity for the therapist presents itself to demonstrate to the family that change is natural, fast and not dependent on more than one member to take the initiative. This is especially important in working with families where the substance abuser is still active and the family is doubtful that a positive change can occur while one family member is abusing alcohol or other drugs. These families are frequently angry at their participation in treatment while the alcoholic or other drug abuser remains uninvolved. The family, of course, needs to be prepared that the addict is likely to increase his abusive behavior temporarily, but is incapable of maintaining this in the family context if the family continues to increase its own repertoire of behaviors. During this phase, much emphasis is placed in therapy on increasing individual and interpersonal resources. NLP postulates that the person with the most choice is in charge of the system and the substance abuser rapidly becomes the least flexible member in the family system once the non-abusing members embrace the possibility of change. In this way, the addict loses control over his family, compelling him in many instances to embrace a more productive lifestyle, if he chooses to remain in the family system. Family members, furthermore, have limited trust in the permanent cessation of abusive behavior — generally this has taken place many times prior to treatment — and need sustaining processes if actual movement toward well being, toward a sense of a healing future is to be established. Neuro-Linguistic Programming, through its specific skills, strategies and techniques, creates rapid access to essential resources in ongoing sobriety and abstinence such as detachment, assertiveness, calmness, patience, perspective, humor, etc., which are a necessity in (re)building a selfsustaining family unit. In addition to working with the family as a whole, NLP directs its variety of treatment processes to the individuals that make up the family. The aforementioned trauma fix is often an essential component to enable the family to proceed as a unit. This strategy allows a traumatized family member to gather the necessary resources for managing a painful life event and move through this trauma, freeing up energy that then may be focused on the family recovery process.

TWO CASE APPLICATIONS

A young couple with one child, married for four years, but together since their sophomore year in high school, had been in family treatment for six months after the husband had completed a twenty-eight day inpatient substance recovery program. Little observable change had taken place and I requested that each adult be seen individually. During the first session, the wife emotionally explained that her husband had raped her several times while under the influence of drugs and alcohol, but that he had no memory of these occasions. She was afraid to tell him about the incidents because she did not know what harm it could cause to the already fragile marriage. Using the NLP trauma fix, the wife began to heal the rape experience, which allowed her to discuss this in the marital sessions. The husband actually did remember the events, and since the wife had become less emotional about the experience because of what she had accomplished on an individual basis, the husband became less threatened and eventually was able to take responsibility for his actions, which had a significant healing effect on the marital relationship.

A second NLP technique, a phobia fix, is often useful in dealing with strongly installed dysfunctional responses to the alcoholic or other substance abuser. Spouses and children of alcoholics may respond to the newly sober and/or abstinent family member in an obsessive-compulsive fashion determined by pre-sobriety demands. For example, a non-alcoholic husband and his three children became panic stricken when the wife and mother, eighteen months into sobriety, was not home for dinner one night, a behavior that in the past had signaled the beginning of an alcoholic episode. All family members were dispatched to the woman's previous familiar drinking places. When the woman called for help because her car had broken down, no one was home to answer her call. The family went into a tailspin, until through the use of the phobia fix, which focuses on increasing choices in feelings and thoughts to change automatic obsessive-compulsive behavior, each family member became competent at accessing more productive behavior, congruent with the newly established state of family sobriety. Neuro-Linguistic Programming recognizes that the unconscious, in a sense, does not keep up with changes in the present and acknowledges that reality is perceived through perceptual lenses, that clients actually judge their present world through the lens of their respective past life experiences.

Personal Processes as Part of the Family System

In the trauma fix as well as the phobia fix NLP focuses the client's unconscious mind on the available resources in the present to eliminate protection from unprocessed past events, which give rise to the trauma-focused or phobic behavior. NLP assists the client in recognizing that what were threatening realities at one time, no longer necessarily need to be approached with behaviors which, in the past, had been designed to cope with these feared events, that in the present the unconscious mind can accept that either the reality has changed or that new skills have been acquired to deal with these threatening realities or both. Addictive families gain understanding of each member's personal processes as part of a larger system and are assisted in pacing and leading effectively, enabling the respective members to increase their choices in behavior toward each other. The resulting resources such as confidence, self worth and self respect allow for increased personal and family flexibility as well as the establishment of personal boundaries. New responses, ones that ecologically move the clientsystem toward well being, take the place of old, dysfunctional automatic responses. NLP perceives much human activity as automatic and seeks to replace dysfunctional automatic responses with new alternatives which become building blocks for the clientsystems' state of well being. Once a family becomes involved in the process of recovery, any systematic change in anchors supports and reinforces the clientsystems' move toward a desired state of health.

CONCLUSION

Families embroiled in an addictive process generally have decreasing options for behavioral responses which leads to a rigid family system. Neuro-Linguistic Programming is designed to install renewed flexibility into the family process by reaccessing and installing resources that move the clientsystem toward well being. NLP presents a variety of techniques for the development of these resources on conscious and unconscious levels, based on a number of presuppositions about human beings and family systems. NLP places great emphasis on the use of rapport skills which the therapist uses to meet the clientsystem in its model of the world and recognizes that this model is determined in families by the collective perceptual lenses of reality. NLP further recognizes that all behavior therefore is purposeful, given the clientsystem's model of the world and that all manifested dysfunctional behavior can be reframed in terms of its original positive intent. In this manner, all behavior makes sense in its original context and is expected to automatically decrease when new, more productive and emotionally less costly responses are accessed. NLP emphasizes on the ecology of newly installed behaviors to create the greatest opportunity for family systems to move towards a compelling future with hope, ease, and a sense of autonomy and selfworth.

REFERENCES

Andreas, S., & Andreas, C. (1987). *Change your mind and keep the change.* Real People Press: Moab, Utah.

Bandler, Richard. (1985). *Using your brain—for a change: Neuro-linguistic programming.* Real People Press: Moab, Utah.

Bandler, R., & Grinder, J. (1979). *Frogs into princes.* Real People Press: Moab, Utah.

Bandler, R., & Grinder, J. (1982). *Re-framing—Neuro-linguistic programming and the transformation of meaning.* Real People Press: Moab, Utah.

Cameron-Bandler, C., Gordon, D., & Lebeau, U. (1985). *Know how: Guided programs for inventing your own best future.* Future Pace, Inc.: San Rafael, CA.

Cameron-Bandler. (1985). *Solutions: Practical and effective antidotes for sexual and relationship problems.* Future Pace, Inc.: San Rafael, CA.

Davis, D. (1980: in press). *Neuro-Linguistic Programming in Alcoholism Treatment.* New York: The Haworth Press, Inc.

Dilts, R. (1983). *Applications of neuro-linguistic programming.* Meta Publications: Cupertino, CA.

Grinder, J., & Bandler, R. (1976). *The structure of magic I: A book about communications and change.* Science and Behavior Books, Inc.: Palo Alto, CA.

Family Therapy
and Twelve-Step Programs:
A Complementary Process

Emily D. Schroeder, MA, CAC

SUMMARY. This paper will illustrate ways in which the basic principles of twelve-step programs and rehabilitation programs for chemical dependency can be combined with systems theory in a complementary way to facilitate the recovery of the members of chemically dependent families.

Family systems therapy offers no magic, but the theory provides a different way for conceptualizing the problem, offering a number of approaches for working with "wet" systems and assisting with new ways to regulate distance and closeness when alcohol or drugs are no longer the major organizing principle (Bowen, 1978).

When rehabilitation programs first began in the early seventies as a form of treatment for alcoholism, there was sometimes a critical attitude from the old timers in AA who had "come into the program off the street." Mental health professionals held a negative, stereotyped attitude towards the alcoholic and a reluctance to acknowledge the importance of the twelve-step recovery approach (Bratter and Forrest, 1985). Over time these attitudes changed: AA became more accepting of the rehabilitation movement; mental health professionals, observing the successes in AA, became curious and began to learn from alcoholism counselors. *Currently, however, there still seems to be resistance among alcoholism professionals and*

Emily D. Schroeder is Executive Director of the Family Systems Network, a private practice, located at 316 Summit Avenue, Summit, NJ and is on the faculty of the Rutgers School of Alcohol Studies.

persons in twelve-step programs to seeing the benefits of systems thinking, a mental health concept, as part of the recovery process.

This paper will make an effort to illustrate how there is a complementarity between twelve-step program concepts and family therapy, where there is similarity with perhaps a separate vocabulary or where family therapy may be different but still useful. Webster's Collegiate Thesaurus (1976), defines complementary as "something that makes up a deficiency; a mutual supplying of each other's lack. Syn: supplement."

In no way does the author intend to make the suggestion that it should be an either/or choice.

Included in the article will be a brief review of the AA movement, the similarities and differences in twelve-step and systems thinking, and the contribution of the mental health field to the understanding of the organization of the family. The issues in "wet" and "dry" systems will be explored.

Also discussed will be how twelve-step programs and family therapy help the individual in the process of differentiation, and ways in which families can work out issues together with the hope of forming new patterns for healthier relationships. What frequently exists in recovery for many families is a mutual isolation.

It will show approaches in different stages of alcoholic family process: the family with active addiction; intervention as a special way of working with the family system to get help for the chemically dependent; and lastly, recommendations for working with the family members in early and later recovery. Although it is idealistic to think that relationships can be healed with all recovering persons, there is the possibility for fewer marital separations and/or increased opportunities for working through some of the issues with the family of origin instead of the customary "cut-offs" that one too often sees in recovering individuals and their families.

The definition we will use for the alcoholic family is the family with chronic alcoholism as the central theme that organizes the family. All members accommodate and adapt to the drinking in some way for the survival of the system (Steinglass, 1987).

For ease of presentation, the pronoun "he" will be used for the alcoholic and "she" for the spouse. This is not to suggest that the reverse is not also an appropriate way to refer to the couple. Although it is possible for both to be alcoholic, this will not be addressed in this paper. The terms "alcoholic" and "chemically dependent" will also be used interchangeably.

THE TWELVE-STEP MOVEMENT

The Twelve-Step Program of Alcoholics Anonymous was the first successful way of helping the alcoholic to stay sober. The analytical approach of the mental health field and the focus on alcoholic drinking as a "symptom" of an underlying problem did not meet with the same positive results, and professionals frequently developed a sense of hopelessness about the alcoholic.

By the end of the eighties, AA and Al-Anon Family Groups had grown tremendously in size and numbers throughout the world. Groups include ACOA and Co-Dependency as well as meetings for other addictions, or persons with common problems. All pattern themselves after the twelve steps of Alcoholics Anonymous. The model works. The focus is on the individual and his or her ability to change.

PROFESSIONAL REHABILITATION PROGRAMS

By the late sixties recovering alcoholics and other concerned professionals developed programs for the rehabilitation of the alcoholic, the best known of which was called the "Minnesota Model." They were based largely on the twelve steps and relied heavily on AA for the continuation of abstinence after treatment. In-patient programs focused on the alcoholic, centering on the individual and his feelings, educating him about alcoholism as a disease, and providing group experiences of sharing and reaching out to others. All of these are critical components in the recovery process. Although there were other methods of treating the alcoholic, the successful programs, in the opinion of this author, were those which prepared the addict for entry into Alcoholics Anonymous. The seventies saw the development of many rehabilitation programs and today professional treatment for the addicted person is plentiful.

Initially there was not much involvement with the family and when that did become part of treatment in the mid seventies, it leaned toward helping the alcoholic in his recovery. This kept the focus of the family on the alcoholism, an already familiar role. The goal was to get family members to Al-Anon, where they would learn to stop their enabling and focus on themselves. It was at least a decade before residential family treatment became an integral part of rehabilitation programs, offering education about alcoholism as a disease, but also helping family members to focus on themselves and their own recovery.

INDIVIDUAL VERSUS SYSTEMS APPROACH IN COUNSELING

The individual approach to counseling tends to be more "linear," or "cause and effect." Most of us begin trying to understand *why* something is happening to us at a very young age. However, Bowen (1974) says that there is the danger that this kind of thinking can lead to a lot of the "blaming" that most of us can get involved with when we are troubled.

By contrast, with systems theory the "focus is on the functional *facts* of relationships. It focuses on *what* happened, *how* it happened, and *when* and *where* it happened insofar as these observations are based on fact" (Bowen, 1974). It carefully avoids what Bowen refers to as "mans automatic preoccupation with *why* it happened." He says that this is one of the main differences between conventional and systems theory" (1974).

Many family people get "stuck" in their own view of their problems. They may be "detached" ("It's not my problem.") but they are frequently caught in the linear "blaming" described above, illustrated by such common statements as, "Don't take my inventory," or, "You're being judgmental." The counselor needs to be aware of not reinforcing that behavior through empathy or "joining" with their complaints and focusing instead on helping them to work through the uncomfortable feelings in order to define their own boundaries and take an "I" position for themselves.

A desired goal for the family systems professional would be to have the recovering family or couple in treatment and also involved in their own twelve-step programs. Family therapy should not be used to the exclusion of or as a replacement for self-help groups. When the drinking stops, estrangement and alienation frequently develop within the family because the members do not know how to connect without the crises that alcohol abuse can create (Berenson, 1976).

In spite of this awareness, professionals in rehabilitation programs and people in twelve-step recovery programs tend not to look at methodologies such as family therapy that can be used in a complementary way to help family members enhance their individual growth. Their comfort level seems to be with the individual approach that focuses on the self in an insular way, giving a more linear perspective on the issues that are confronting the person.

By contrast, family therapists focus on the individual *within* the family. It is helpful to have the family or couple together in counseling, but whether the individual, couple, or whole family attends the session is not the key issue; it is how the counselor sees the dynamics and repetitious patterns that exist around the problems as he or she listens and observes.

TWELVE-STEP PROGRAMS AND RESPONSIBILITY FOR SELF

The steps of AA and other Twelve-Step programs are as follows:

Step One: "Admitted we were powerless over alcohol — that our lives had become unmanageable."

Step Two: "Came to believe that a Power greater than ourselves could restore us to sanity."

Step Three: "Made a decision to turn our will and our lives over to the care of God *as we understood him.*"

These three steps say that the individual cannot be rid of the obsession for alcohol until he *takes responsibility for his powerlessness* and the unmanageability of his life. This is an amazing paradox. He then has to *believe* that a Power greater than himself can help him which involves *trusting* someone other than himself, and he has to *make a decision* to turn himself and his life over to that Power.

Step Four:	"Made a searching and fearless moral inventory of ourselves."
Step Five:	"Admitted to God, to ourselves, and to another human being the exact nature of our wrongs."
Step Six:	"Were entirely ready to have God remove all these defects of character."
Step Seven:	"Humbly asked him to remove our shortcomings."
Step Eight:	"Made a list of all persons we had harmed, and became willing to make amends to them all."
Step Nine:	"Made direct amends to such people wherever possible except where to do so would injure them or others."
Step Ten:	"Continue to take personal inventory and when we were wrong promptly admitted it."
Step Eleven:	"Sought through prayer and meditation to improve our conscious contact with God as we understood Him, praying only for knowledge of His will for us and the power to carry that out."
Step Twelve:	"Having had a spiritual awakening as the result of these steps, we tried to carry this message to alcoholics, and to practice these principles in all our affairs."

These nine other steps encourage the individual to continue to look at himself on an ongoing basis, sharing "shortcomings" with his Higher Power and another human being, and to continue to take responsibility for the consequences of his actions in his personal relationships. The final step speaks about actively reaching out to others and live a meaningful life in all one's affairs (*Twelve Steps and Twelve Traditions*, 1987).

TWELVE-STEP THINKING AND SYSTEMS THINKING

The *Big Book of Alcoholics Anonymous* (1978) says, "Rarely have we seen a person fail who has thoroughly followed our path." The first three steps suggest that our own human resources of knowledge, strength and hope are not enough at times to solve our problems and we must *recognize* and *accept* the need for Someone or Something outside of ourselves to guide us in a workable partnership (*Al-Anon's Twelve Steps and Twelve Traditions*, 1988). Turning our will and our lives over to that Power involves taking responsibility for "letting go." The manifestation of that Power in our lives may differ for each of us, and change as we grow in recovery. If indeed that Power is reaching us through the help of someone else, it is perhaps a miracle that we cannot see until we have the growth within ourselves that allows us to comprehend a larger concept.

Twelve-step programs suggest that the individual has to take care of his or her own well being and not become trapped in the enmeshment of others. By going to meetings, the person is getting the "separateness" from toxic situations and the support that is needed to maintain sobriety and/or make changes.

The systems thinking of Murray Bowen (1978) suggests that as long as people are "undifferentiated" from others and continue the enmeshment that their role in the family demands they cannot experience fully the growth potential that is within their capabilities. Optimal family development is thought to take place when family members are relatively differentiated and each has developed a sense of self, when anxiety is low, and when the parents are in good emotional contact with their own families of origin (Nichols, 1984).

It is a step towards maturation and differentiation when we begin to "act" for ourselves instead of "reacting" to others. This manner of managing our lives relates to what Al-Anon calls "detachment."

THE TWELVE-STEP GROUP AS A METAPHOR
OF AN OPEN FAMILY SYSTEM

The power of the group is built into the twelve-step programs: people who are recovering from the same problems have experience, strength and hope to share together. They are in an "open" environment where there is trust and safety, where the members of the group can learn new attitudes and behaviors that allow them to find comfort. Paradoxically, however, the twelve-step group also has boundaries that seem to make it a "closed" system, which, by definition, is a group where only those with the same issues would feel comfortable and "outsiders" don't "fit."

Members of these programs frequently come from families that are also "closed" systems, but they have been taught that sharing, feeling, trusting are not options for them and in their families "outsiders" may not "fit." The safety of the twelve-step program permits them to be open with one another. Their common bond allows a healing that comes from surrender to the disease over which they have been powerless and they develop an understanding and acceptance of others in the "fellowship."

Families with chemical dependency have established patterns of interaction that are difficult to change. Some are generations old. The cultural backgrounds from one's family of origin usually create loyalty issues and one's role in the family is such that to change one's ways is to experience guilt. Families can vacillate between feeling powerful and powerless when there is chemical dependency, but they don't know where they fit because of this new program that seems to have taken over their family members. They often feel a powerlessness and abandonment.

The cohesiveness and loyalty in the fellowship of twelve-step programs can be compared to families in that it too can be powerful. However, although these programs offer to members an acceptance of new behavior that allows them to find comfort in a sober life, these changes often are alienating to the family values and appear to be "selfish." The family feels the pressure of isolation and little connection with their recovering person. The recovering chemically dependent person feels "safe" to share only with members of his group.

If the significant others are involved in their own twelve-step family program, they may feel the identification with others that brings some comfort, but still experience the lack of connectedness and the loneliness of living with a person who, in his sobriety, seems strange to them.

Families struggle between a desire to maintain stability and a desire to grow (Steinglass, 1987). Over time they develop a balance about this in their family which systems theory calls *homeostasis*, or keeping the family on an even keel. In the dysfunctional family that has organized its balance around drinking crises, the need for stability becomes more urgent and growth is minimal. They often get "stuck" moving from one stage of the family life cycle to another because this requires change.

The family systems counselor can design ways for the family to see that the twelve-step group is a metaphor for the "healthy family." Twelve-step tradition puts principles before personality while recognizing the need for individual liberty. There is the potential for growth through the openness of its community and the honesty of confrontation and sharing (*Twelve Steps and Twelve Traditions*, 1987).

DISENGAGEMENT VERSUS DIFFERENTIATION IN TWELVE-STEP PROGRAMS

As was stated above, some individuals in their twelve-step programs have become emotionally too distant from their significant others and have no way to connect. Because of their fear of getting close, they use the program to keep apart, much as they may have used alcohol to keep the distance in the past. They could well benefit from family or couples therapy.

What looks like a "differentiated" posture is actually a reactive, pseudo-position. They are, in fact, *disengaged* from their families or spouses, not connecting, which is the opposite of *enmeshed*, or every close. In the early years of sobriety it is a legitimate way to be "separate" while they work on themselves. However, daily attendance at meetings can become a way of avoiding the process of change which leads to healthier relationships and a new homeostatic balance for the family.

ALCOHOL AS A PRIMARY ORGANIZING PRINCIPLE IN FAMILIES

When two people marry they have to make decisions about the lifestyle they are going to have. The couple must clearly delineate what their external and internal boundaries will be and work to develop a set of shared beliefs, values and guidelines or "rules" for living together (Steinglass, 1987). This generally comes about through situations that occur early in the marriage and requires them to make a decision about what is acceptable behavior on the part of each. Their life experience to date in their family of origin gives them their opinions about any given issue. There are many variants involved: what each learned from living in his or her respective families, whether each wants the resolution to be handled in the same manner as their parents or the opposite, and whether they agree or disagree with each other about this (Steinglass, 1987).

Alcohol is one of the key issues that arises. What are the expectations about drinking? If both are from a family where there were similar values about use of alcohol there is likely to be merging of their thinking. However, one might come from a similar background but say, in essence, "I want it to be *different* from the way it was in my family" and the new mate does not agree. Or they may both be in agreement, because of the pain of early experiences with alcohol in their families of origin, take a *reactive* position of abstinence, and in later years be shocked when alcoholism emerges in the next generation. There is also the possibility that one might come from a background with a different attitude than the spouse about drinking, and object to frequency of drinking incidents, amounts consumed, with whom one drinks, and where drinking occurs. Some couples separate at this early stage of the marriage when there is abuse of substances and no agreement about the role of alcohol in the marriage. However, this is more likely to occur when the disagreeing partner comes from a family where alcohol consumption has not been a key issue (Steinglass, 1987).

The formation of the alcoholic family begins in early marriage around the issue of drinking and ultimately it becomes *the principle organizing theme in the family*. Over time the spouse dyad becomes one of over and under responsibility as the marital balance (Bowen,

1973; Steinglass, 1987). Why do so many marriages occur where drinking is in the family of origin of each? It is common to see children of alcoholics marrying alcoholics, becoming alcoholics or both. Murray Bowen (1978), a pioneer of systems theory, states that "people find someone to have a primary relationship with where each has about the same level of differentiation."

In 1973 at an on alcoholic family seminar in Durham, N.C. Bowen said,

> Why are people who work with alcoholism slower than most in going over to family? I am pleased that we are accepting the notion that the family is important in alcoholism.
>
> The family is a system, and a change in the functioning of one family member is automatically followed by a compensatory change in the other family member. Systems theory focuses on the functioning of the system. In other words, anytime you have a sick member of the system, you have a person who is overfunctioning in relation to this one. As long as the overfunctioner keeps overfunctioning, and they stay in relationship, the underfunctioner stays down.

WET AND DRY SYSTEMS

A "wet system" is one in which the alcoholic continues to drink problematically, and a "dry system" is one where active drinking is not a problem but the family's problems continue (Bratter and Forrest, 1985). While alcoholism professionals focus on the "wet" and "dry" states of the chemically dependent person, the family therapist focuses more on the existing reactive patterns during these two periods.

In the alcoholic family every member of the family plays an adaptive role when the alcoholic drinks. The family does not have a conscious choice about the selection of adapting patterns. It was "programmed" into the spouses by their parents (Bowen, 1987). Their behavioral patterns are predictable; boundaries are either rigid or unclear and communication is skewed. The family focus is on the chemically dependent person who has a compulsive need to drink or use mood altering chemicals. It is the use of the alcohol or drugs that organizes the family. With the progression of the drinking the family isolates more and more from their social environment. Secrets prevail within the family. I would consider an assessment incomplete if I had not heard someone say in a session, "I never knew that."

All have the goal of abstinence for the chemically dependent person. However, the interactions of the alcoholic individual and the family while drinking is the *key* the systems therapist will use to help resolve the drinking problem (Berenson, 1976).

Contrary to the opinion of many professionals, the "dry" state presents *more* tension because of the lack of stability in the system. Family members express themselves during drinking episodes in a way that they cannot when the drinking stops. Berenson (1976) lists the following differences between these two states, saying that the ultimate goal is a synthesis of them:

DRY	WET
Nonexperiencing	Overexperiencing
Objective	Subjective
Overresponsible	Underresponsible
Boring	Exciting
Reasonable	Irrational
Polite, unassertive	Angry, aggressive
Use of willpower	Impulsive
No sex	Sex or excuse not to have sex
Modest	Boasting
Stoical	Maudlin

Berenson (Kaufman, 1984) uses an adaptation of Bowen's systems model, viewing the treatment of the alcoholic and his family as progressing in three stages which are related to issues of closeness and distance. In the first stage, termed "wet stage," the goals are (1) to get the family to pull together; (2) to get the spouse to focus on her "I" position from her position of overresponsibility; (3) to get her to Al-Anon for a support system and (4) to achieve an alcohol free state. Since the alcoholic is dependent on the predictable reactions of his family to his drinking episodes, he will become uncomfortable with the change and is likely to "hit bottom."

Berenson terms the second stage *adaptation to sobriety*, a period during which intimacy is discouraged until the family system organizes without alcohol. The third stage he calls *maintenance* or restoration of spousal intimacy. Counseling during each of these stages could involve up to six to twelve months. The therapist should be pleased with gradual improvement (Kaufman, 1984) remembering that old patterns of action and reaction are "programmed" from early childhood and do not change easily.

FAMILY WITH ACTIVE CHEMICAL DEPENDENCY

One tends to observe different views among members of twelve-step programs, alcoholism professionals and systems therapists about intervening in a family where there is active chemical dependency. *Nevertheless, all have a common goal: to get the alcoholic or drug addict to stop using.* Closer examination, however, suggests that it is in the timing and the process that there is disagreement. The twelve-step program, as was stated earlier, sees the person as having to "hit bottom." The alcoholism professional wants the family therapist directly to approach the person with the abuse problem with the intention of "stopping his use." Although this puts the alcoholic on the defensive and seldom works, it seems to continue to be a fixed view of many in that profession. The family therapist sees the problem in the system; that is, in the way the family's adaptation to the drinking episodes has set up patterns that perpetuate the problem. This is in keeping with the belief that alcohol or drugs become a central organizing theme in families where there is addiction.

Nevertheless, it *is* important in the first session to evaluate the extent of substance abuse/dependence as well as the difficulties it presents for the family (Kaufman, 1984). However, Berenson (1976) states that it is not helpful to label the problem alcoholism (even if the family does so). In this he concurs with AA that it is better for each individual himself to make that determination. He wants to desensitize the subject of drinking and encourage open discussion.

The therapist perceives how the family and the alcoholic interact while drinking. For the systems counselor, this is the key to helping to resolve the drinking problem. The behavior of the alcoholic when drinking and the adaptive, reinforcing behaviors expressed by the significant others are not present when there is not drinking. The professional counselor looks at the way the family is organized, focusing more on process, in order to assist the members in changing their part in the repetitive patterns of that process.

Systems thinkers concur that all behavior is somehow protective of the system. Elaine Rosenfeld in her article, "Systemic Family Therapy and the Treatment of Intoxication, Abstinence and Recovery," says that asking certain questions of the family helps to define the homeostatic role that alcohol has played in maintaining the family system. The challenge is to see what alcohol allows the alcoholic to do, what it allows others to do. Who profits from the intoxicated behavior; what does the intoxicated behavior make possible; how would others be required to change if the alcoholic stopped drinking?

According to Berenson, power is almost a useless concept in the alcoholic family system because both the chemically dependent person and the spouse both feel powerless in their attempts to control each other (1976) even though the marriage is generally a complementary one of under/overfunctioning (Bowen, 1974).

He also emphasizes that whenever one maintains therapy with a "wet" alcoholic or drug abuser, the therapist has the responsibility of *not maintaining the illusion that a family is resolving problems while in fact it is really reinforcing them* (Kaufman, 1984). His goals are (1) to cool down the system by reducing the emotional entanglement or fusion and (2) not to pursue the alcoholic. Attempting to get through to the alcoholic would be duplicating the (unsuccessful) patterns that have been used by family members and is therefore unproductive. If the alcoholic is resistant, the counselor can give him the choice of coming or not coming to sessions and work with the spouse. Goals would be to develop trust, assist her in seeing her contribution to the process (Kaufman and Kaufmann, 1979) and to look at and work on her own "emptiness" or lack of "self."

If treatment does not progress with the alcoholic couple, it is sometimes wiser to see the spouse alone. The family therapist needs to encourage her to go to Al-Anon as a support system so that all the intensity is not channelled into the individual therapy sessions (Berenson, 1976). The coaching that says "stop being so responsible for others," "don't rescue," "detach," "don't enable," is often impossible for the spouse at first and she can only take a "pseudo-position" because family rules, often handed down through many generations, say that change in the way one does things is not acceptable if you are a "loyal" family member.

To get beyond the impasse created by the family loyalty issues that impede change, the therapist can *reframe* "change" as a way to "help" the alcoholic. "What can you do that's different?" This is a strategic technique that involves the therapist's expressing a view that implies what looks like negative behavior can be seen as positive (Treadway, 1989). It offers the person a "new map" for making changes.

The systems therapist sees the non-alcoholic as the main leverage in the "wet" system (Berenson, 1976). The non-alcoholic spouse is generally the more functional and possibly the more motivated. This person is encouraged to take more responsibility for self with what Bowen calls an "I" position (1978), and become less enmeshed with the alcoholic. The idea is for the non-alcoholic spouse to "hit bottom" first by recognizing the emptiness inside herself and working on that. As she distances from the situation, the alcoholic usually gets worse. If the spouse does not get pulled back into the fused position, the alcoholic often will take his turn, "hit bottom" and stop drinking.

Berenson suggests that professionals who are counseling with the spouses of chemically dependent persons can listen to their "story" and offer three choices: (1) keep on doing exactly what you are doing; (2) emotionally remove yourself from the situation; (3) physically leave home (Kaufman & Kaufmann, 1979). *Whatever the choice, the decision* is theirs, and therefore they are taking responsibility for themselves. Written tasks can be given to document how they carry out their decision. This allows them initially to continue to overfunction in a different way and to begin to see more clearly the effects of their adaptive behaviors. Subsequent sessions can lead them towards new changes for themselves.

Bowen (1974) states that there is one basic principle that applies to any family in which one significant family member is in a marked overfunctioning position and the other a marked dysfunctioning position.

It is far easier to help the overfunctioning person tone down the overfunctioning than it is to try to help the dysfunctional one increase the functioning. In any situation in which there is an either-or choice of where to put the focus in therapy sessions, it is with the overfunctioning family member.

INTERVENTION AS A PROCESS

One of the areas where Twelve-Step programs and the alcoholism or systems professionals may differ is that of intervening with the alcoholic in order to "create a bottom" (helping him to see the reality of his alcoholism) and getting him to treatment. AA tends to think that the alcoholic has to "hit bottom" on his own. In this process, the counselor works with the family and concerned others giving them education about the disease of alcoholism and the dynamics involved in the alcoholic system. There are discussions about how the drinking has affected *them*. This allows expression of feelings in an open environment and can lead to detoxification of their anger and blaming and to ease their pain. Finally, they have a session with the chemically dependent person. The goal is to express their pain and concerns in a *receivable* way and ask him or her to get help. They also give their "bottom line" statement if that person refuses treatment.

Intervention can be seen as a systems approach, because it is based on the concept that a family system is more powerful than any individual; the process shifts power from the alcoholic to the family as a unit. It empowers the family when they, as individuals, have felt powerless. They have more strength and potential to reach the alcoholic *together* than they had in any individual efforts.

The openness of expression redefines the "no talk" rule, and in breaking through the family's denial, it unbalances the system. Subsystems that might not have had open communication begin to talk. Just the fact that the intervention *occurs* shifts power within the family. This is provided in an arena where the common goal is treatment and sobriety. It is an intensive process, taking several hours of preparation before confronting the chemically dependent family member, and it has a high rate of success.

It is the opinion of this author that intervention as a process needs a family systems approach for follow-up along with Al-Anon because the process *does* unbalance a system that has many years of established dysfunctional communication patterns. It frequently cannot sustain the stress of change, and members unconsciously try to return to the familiar homeostatic balance.

Information about intervention is well documented in the literature (Johnson, 1973, 1988; Maxwell, 1976).

FAMILY THERAPY IN EARLY SOBRIETY

A key question in early sobriety is, "how do families organize without active addiction as a central organizing theme?" A primary goal is to decrease the emotional distance without having the drinking resume (Berenson, 1976). In order to have an atmosphere that is conducive to the growth of individuals and where alcohol no longer "fits," everyone must make changes. If, as was suggested earlier, the family's primary organizing principle is alcohol, it must no longer have a position of power in the family's organization. It is not unusual during this time for depression to develop in the spouse, signifying the "emptiness" in her after the years of focusing on the alcoholic rather than her own needs (Berenson, 1979).

The chemically dependent person if frequently advised to go to "90 meetings in 90 days," or to attend a twelve-step program at least as frequently as he used chemicals. Family members are encouraged to go to Al-Anon family groups. Many professionals are in agreement that to accomplish this can be a challenging task for the therapist unless the spouse's involvement in Al-Anon precedes the partner's entry into a recovery program. It is not unusual for the spouse to see the alcoholism as "his problem," thus denying the interactional patterns that help perpetuate the drinking. Counselors may hear the complaint, "I liked him better when he drank." Unless the spouse was a "drinking partner" this statement refers more to the unpredictability of the "dry system" that has replaced the predictability of the "wet" system (Berenson, 1976). There are no stable patterns without alcohol as the central theme. No one knows what to do.

The following is an example of the circular movement in chemically dependent families between "wet" and "dry," and how tension is relieved by returning to the "wet" stage where family roles are familiar (see Figure 1).

It is not common practice with alcoholism professionals to have family or couples therapy in the early days of recovery, but there are sound advantages to including this as part of the treatment plan. A therapist working with a recovering couple, however, needs to have an understanding of the role alcohol and/or drugs have played in the family dynamics.

It is a time to help couples or family members "connect" in ways that are safe. This could take many forms: it could be working with them as individuals but in the presence of the other. Dysfunctional families have thrived in secrecy and the arena of the family therapy sessions provides a certain safety to become more open. It is not a time for frequent sessions, nor to do "therapy" as such. Rather, it is a time to help keep the system calm while it goes through the changes to a new homeostatic balance that is conducive to individual growth.

Although it is sometimes a "pink cloud" stage, family members soon realize that all the dreams and hopes they had about "if only the drinking stopped" are little more than fantasies. The fact is that life is either chaotic or boring, and their fantasies are not becoming reality without alcohol or drugs in their lives. It is a time when the family has *no way to connect*. Too much anxiety can create a "relapse" which would allow the family to play their predictable roles and thus restore the familiar homeostatic balance.

Seeing families or couples in early recovery could be "one on one" counseling working with individual members (in the presence of the others) exploring facts about their families of origin or looking at past patterns of interaction from other generations. If those issues are too toxic and create emotional tension, however, it is not appropriate at this time.

Sessions could repeat information about the affects of the disease. It could involve short term problem solving where you, the therapist, are providing guidance. It could be warning them that

FIGURE 1

REPETITIVE CYCLES OF WET/DRY STAGES
OF CHEMICALLY DEPENDENT FAMILIES

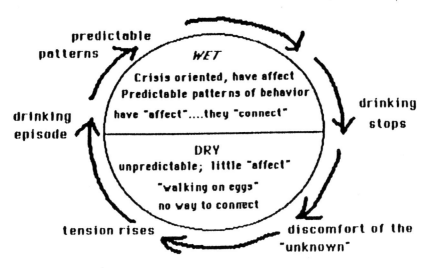

David Berenson, M.D.

A goal of therapy can be helping families to have the
qualities of the "wet" stage without crisis of chemicals

getting emotional is asking for trouble. Talking in the sessions
through the therapist is safer than direct contact in these early days
of recovery. Couples can be directed to "restrain from changing"
around issues where they need to be distant. This can give them
permission to be comfortable about where they are, and it may work
paradoxically in that restraint and positive connotation of it allows
them to get close. Collaborating *together* to achieve this "distance"
is by definition "closeness" (Treadway, 1989).

The treatment plan needs to keep each of them in their respective
self-help groups getting a sense of self as an individual rather than
the enmeshed or disengaged states they have had in their family

life. At the same time the therapist works with them slowly in ways to help them to safely connect.

FAMILY THERAPY IN LATER SOBRIETY

The goal of Bowen's therapy is increased differentiation of self. According to him nothing else lasts. Genuine change in the family system requires the reopening of closed family ties and detriangulation, which creates the conditions for individual autonomy and growth (Nichols, 1984). Patterns in families are repeated from generation to generation. For example, distancing as a way to avoid the tension in one's family of origin will again be repeated in the marital or other primary relationships as tension mounts.

One of the options for couples in later recovery is to begin to work on family of origin relationships, and to "step out of the middle" of toxic triangles in which they are caught emotionally between two persons whose issues are other than their own. "Coaching" from the therapist can lead to new ways to communicate with their parents or other family members. Bowen states that emotional cut-offs that one sees in the alcoholic family are often a *denial* of the importance of the family and their attitude is only an exaggerated facade of independence (Nichols, 1984).

Gradually the therapist can move the couple towards taking risks to become more intimate in their relationship with each other. If it is too soon, the effort will create tension that will be the signal that they are not ready to move toward spousal intimacy. Tasks can be designed to develop ways of having fun without drinking (Kaufman, 1985). They can work at this stage on resolution of the past, forgiving themselves instead of blaming (Treadway, 1989).

Often the couple want to terminate counseling before reaching this stage of therapy. When this happens, it may be a sign that they have progressed as much as they can at this point, and they need to be encouraged to continue their active twelve-step involvement. Berenson believes that if they have established a good rapport with the therapist, they will return at a later date if they are having particular problems with an acting out child, for example, or are motivated to continue their family of origin work and/or their efforts becoming more intimate with each other (Berenson, 1976).

CONCLUSION

There are advantages to being involved in family systems counseling in addition to twelve step involvement. AA, Al-Anon and other twelve-step groups help individuals to take care of themselves and to "differentiate" or take an "I" position but there is often a distance and reluctance to take a "we" position in their relationships. Family therapy can focus at the appropriate times on either the individuals or the relationship.

There are now couples groups in twelve-step programs; Al-Anon and AA often meet in the same churches at the same time; there are anniversaries where speakers are present from AA, Al-Anon and Alateen.

Family or couples therapy can further facilitate individual growth by working separately with the alcoholic and spouse but in front of the other. This allows a safe way of gaining knowledge about the other person. In later sobriety, secrets could come out that previously existed through the protectiveness of poor communication channels in the family. This helps to lessen the distance that so frequently becomes a problem in recovery.

A client was asked by the author to share how she thought family systems counseling was helpful to her in her marriage. Her husband had at that time four years in AA and she 12 years in Al-Anon. She said,

> I felt our marriage was going nowhere. Our family members were more comfortable with one another but we were distant from each other. I learned that I was the 'pursuer' and he the 'distancer.' I was tired of having 'conversations' with him in my head because to do otherwise made him walk away from me.
>
> In Al-Anon I learned that I could change no one but myself, but in family therapy I was taught that I could express myself in a way that might enable Bill to hear me without feeling threatened, and in so doing this could allow him to hear, think, and decide whether or not he wanted to change. I also learned that I could not expect others to give me what they did not have. I lowered my expectations and was much better able to

accept my husband and the members of my family the way they are. I feel it adds a lot to my fellowship of Al-Anon.

— Mary N, July, 1990

REFERENCES

Alcoholics Anonymous. (1976). *Alcoholics Anonymous: The basic text for alcoholics anonymous.* New York: World Services Organization, Third Edition, new and revised, p. 58.

Al-Anon. (1988). *Al-Anon's twelve steps and twelve traditions.* New York: Al-Anon Family Group Headquarters, Inc., p. 13.

Bepko, Claudia with Jo Ann Krestan, *The Responsibility trap: A blueprint for treating the alcoholic family.* New York: The Free Press, Macmillan, Inc., 1985.

Berenson, D. (1976). "Alcohol and the Family System." In P. J. Guerin (Ed.), *Family therapy: Theory and practice.* (pp. 287-293). New York: Gardner Press, 287, 288, 291, 292, 293.

———— (1979). "The therapist's relationship with couples with an alcoholic member. In E. Kaufman, P. Kaufman (Eds.). *Family therapy of drug and alcohol abuse.* (pp. 235-239). New York: Gardner Press. pgs. 235, 238, 239.

Bowen, M. (1978). *Family therapy in clinical practice.* New York: Aronson.

————. (1974). *Addictions, 21*(2), 4-11.

Bratter, T., & Forrest, G. (1985). *Alcoholism and substance abuse: Strategies for clinical intervention.* New York: Macmillan and Co.

Carter, E. (1977). Generation after generation. In Papp, P. (Ed.), *Family Therapy: Full Length Case Studies.* New York: Gardner Press, 1977.

Elkin, D. (1984). *Families under the influence.* New York: W.W. Norton & Co.

Johnson, V. (1973). *I'll quit tomorrow.* New York: Harper and Row.

————. (1986). *Intervention: How to help someone who doesn't want help.* Minneapolis: Johnson Institute.

Kaufman, E. (1984). *Substance abuse and family therapy.* New York: Grune and Stratton.

———— (1985). Family therapy in the treatment of alcoholism. In T. Bratter, G. Forrest, (Eds.), *Alcoholism and substance abuse: Strategies for clinical intervention.* New York; MacMillan.

Nichols, M. (1984). *Family therapy: concepts and methods.* New York: Gardner Press.

Robertson, N. (1988). *Getting better: Inside Alcoholics Anonymous.* New York: William Morrow and Co.

Rosenfeld, E.S. Systemic family therapy and the treatment of intoxication, abstinence and recovery. In *Social Work Treatment of Alcohol Problems.*

Schultz, S. (1984). *Family Systems Therapy: An integration.* New York.

Steinglass, P, with Bennett, Wolin, and Reiss. (1987). *The alcoholic family*. New York: Basic Books, Inc.

Treadway, D. (1989). *Before it's too late: Working with substance abuse in the family*. New York: W.W. Norton & Co.

_____ (1985). Workshop, Community Mental Health Services Continuing Education, College of Medicine and Dentistry of New Jersey.

Twelve Steps and Twelve Traditions. (1987). New York: Alcoholics Anonymous World Services, Inc.

Addicted Women: Their Families' Effect on Treatment Outcome

Carolann Kane-Cavaiola, MA, CAS
Diane Rullo-Cooney, MA, CAC, CAS

SUMMARY. It is widely known in the addiction treatment community that addicted women present themselves for services in the later stages of chemical dependency and with more complications than their male counterparts. The purpose of this article is to discuss the additional challenges the spouse and children present to the recovering woman in the therapeutic as well as the practical sense.

The addiction treatment field has a varied approach to treating chemically dependent individuals. Most often care is provided in settings that mix male and female populations, making it difficult to focus on the special needs of women early in recovery. Family involvement is generally limited or nonexistent. Consequently, success rates have been less than gratifying. Researchers have established that the onset of a woman's addiction usually is a reaction to a significant life crisis rather than an essential, steady and progres-

Carolann Kane-Cavaiola is Director of the Center for Drug and Alcohol Prevention and Treatment of JFK Medical Center in Edison, NJ. She is co-author of *Basics of Adolescent Development for the Chemical Dependency Professional* and *Continuing Care for the Chemically Dependent Adolescent: Aftercare or Afterthought*. Diane Rullo-Cooney is Clinical Supervisor at the Center for Drug and Alcohol Prevention and Treatment of JFK Medical Center in Edison, NJ. She directs women's services, including primary care, codependency and the family therapy program.

sive pattern, which is the most common in the chemically dependent male (Herrington, Jacobsen, Benger 1987). This "reactive" rather than "essential" explanation of the onset of addiction must be explored in the early recovery process to engage the addicted woman and her family successfully.

PERSPECTIVES ON WOMEN AND ADDICTION

Chemically dependent women of past generations were stereotyped as immoral, poor mothers, and inadequate wives. Research suggests that attitudes continue to be more severe towards female intoxication than male intoxication. Stafford and Pitway (1977) reported that female drunkenness was rated as "more hopeless" than male drunkenness. Sandmaier (1980) reports there is greater social stigma attached to women's addiction than to their male counterpart because notions of acceptable drinking and drugging behaviors are more narrowly and rigidly defined for women. This difference in societal perception may be a result of some real differences between chemically dependent men and women. The amount and degree to which the differences occur has not been fully identified. Bourne and Light (1979) outline some differences:

- Women usually begin drinking (and problem drinking) at a later age than do their male counterparts.
- Women move more rapidly from the early to the later stages of drinking than men do.
- Women, more often will cite a specific stress or traumatic event that precipitated their problem drinking.
- Women appear to do more solitary drinking.
- Female alcoholics are more likely to have affective (emotional) problems (males are more likely to be sociopathic in connection to their addiction).
- Women feel the consequences more often in the family situation.
- Women alcoholics are more likely to be divorced.
- Women get sicker earlier and develop health problems associated with alcohol abuse more rapidly.

— Alcoholic women are frequently characterized as having feelings of guilt, depression, or anxiety that inhibit their functioning.

The addicted woman is viewed as "weak willed, potentially or actively promiscuous and sexually aggressive" (McGuire, 1975). They continue to live under different societal standards. It is generally accepted today, for women to frequent clubs and bars and become involved with drinking and drug use. However, it is highly unacceptable for a woman to become an alcoholic or drug addicted. In an effort to hide their addiction and therefore avoid the stigma it has become common for women to present to the general practitioner their symptoms of nerves, anxiety, or minor depression which then results in a prescription. The female addict will become addicted to this medication. The primary problem of the addiction continues not to be addressed.

Generally, women have been seen as the family caretakers. Their role is to make sure that the children are well fed, and the home clean and the "family business" in order. It is presumed addicted women are unable to function in the role society has set for them. In contrast to this belief, the majority of chemically dependent women are functioning in a work setting, running households, or both.

Due to the stigma of being a chemically dependent female, women do not seek treatment as quickly as men do. They are more reluctant to reveal their inability to control their use, since they share the belief that their home and family should not have to make due without them. The perceived negative consequences to the system supercede her personal need for intervention and treatment.

Being aware of the prejudice surrounding chemically dependent women will help us understand the effects families have on those women who enter treatment. In general health care practices, addicted women are routinely misdiagnosed as having psychiatric or medical problems rather than addictive disorders (Corrigan, 1985). Professionals are not exempt from society's difficulty in recognizing women as being chemically dependent. This could explain some of the over representation of women in mental health and medical practices for nonspecific and vague complaints.

CASE HISTORIES

As professionals know, recovery from addiction is a long term process that requires a high degree of energy and commitment. The case studies will illustrate the challenge that the family presents to quality recovery, and the importance of family treatment.

Case 1

Emily is a 44 year old, white Anglo American, married with three children. Alcohol was the major focus in Emily's life. Treatment was sought because Emily hated being drunk all day. She realized her family was getting embarrassed by her behavior. Not unusual in Anglo American families members go for help only when the problem is serious and after their efforts to solve it themselves have failed or denial of its importance is impossible (McGill & Pearce 1982). Emily lacked any social support. Typical in the Anglo American family, women are forced into relatively isolated dependency (McGill & Pearce 1982). Her drinking was done daily from the time she awakened. She decided, against medical advice, to detoxify herself at home and then attend outpatient treatment. Typical in Anglo American families, one denies, carries on, and above all, takes responsibility for ones problems by not complaining or involving other people (McGill & Pearce 1982).

Initially her children and her husband were pleased with the sober Emily. They were now able to enjoy family activities without being embarrassed by a drunk. A few months into Emily's sobriety the children began displaying behavioral problems. The oldest daughter became angry with her because she would display concern about her activities. The second daughter was arrested for possession of a weapon, and the youngest daughter displayed signs of becoming socially inhibited and introverted.

Emily's husband blamed the disruption and confusion in the family on her. He then increased their social activities by taking her to restaurants or other places where drinking was included. He would become angry if she didn't order a drink. He explained to Emily that periodic drinking at dinner would not affect her, and she needed to learn how to control her drinking. Emily began questioning her alcoholism. The children pointed out her ability to abstain as proof of her misdiagnosis. Emily and her family reverted to active denial. Needless to say the family fought hard, at Emily's cost, to recapture the homeostasis that was most comfortable, Emily began drinking regularly and left treatment.

Discussion

With this population it has been discovered that the addicted wife will overtly experience resistance from her husband when the prospect of treatment is introduced. Beckman and Amaro (1986) found that women find less support for entering treatment in their social and family environment than men do. In Emily's case the family was unable to take a back seat to treatment. Their resentment needed addressing in the therapeutic setting so it would not interfere with early recovery goals. Conversely, as reported by Father Martin (1990), female codependents interfere with recovery much later in the treatment process than male codependents, when the concept of recovery has time to be internalized and important to the addict.

As her spouse played out the role of codependency Emily became the "martyr." As is common in cases where the husband is also using alcohol or drugs, messages are frequently given that it is okay and often required to drink or do drugs with him. It wasn't until Emily's intoxication interfered with his needs that the pattern became unacceptable. This phenomenon is well known to addiction professionals as the addicted family system.

Case 2

Maggie is a 29 year old, Irish woman, married with two sons, ages 8 and 5. She married at 19 years old and her addiction escalated. Maggie's husband did not complain about her drug use initially. In Irish families when the woman's drinking gets out of hand, it is extremely embarrassing for the family, more so since women are supposed to be the strong ones in the family (McGoldrick 1982). As long as she was submissive to all his desires he continued to enable her. In the following seven years, Maggie's addiction flourished. Since she was running their business and keeping her household in order, Maggie's husband did not complain about the drug use.

When Maggie's husband discovered she was having an affair, they reached the crisis point. He immediately blamed her drug use and demanded she get into treatment.

Four months into recovery, her family displayed intense anger. They had not expected Maggie to be so concerned about herself and her sobriety. They thought she would continue to be compliant to their demands but still maintaining her recovery. Maggie's children became defiant and distanced themselves further from her. The children were frightened of losing her. They were upset every time she went out to a self-help meeting, thinking she wasn't coming back. Maggie's husband was frightened by her independence and began pushing Maggie towards making a stronger commitment to their relationship.

The children's problems continued to increase. They both presented with many physical complaints. Their school work suffered as a result of the change in the family system. The family was splitting, the children taking sides with each parent at different times. The children were confused, not knowing which parent to trust. They had a fear of their father and didn't want to lose their mother, they feared a pending divorce.

Maggie's children were seen in a treatment group for children of substance abusers. Her husband refused treatment, stating that the treatment was the cause for the drastic change in Maggie. Maggie remained abstinent. She was struggling with her own development and identity.

Discussion

Maggie was afraid to make a total commitment to her husband and family; she wanted to avoid any possibility of rejection. She did not want to be married and didn't think she would be able to be independent. Due to this instability, Maggie was not making any definitive progress.

The woman is known to be the nurturer, therefore family members resist nurturing the adult woman, they continue however in their efforts to protect then punish. Maggie's family was angry at her involvement outside the home. They described treatment programs or twelve-step groups, as not giving "advice" that was in "her" best interest. The family knew better.

Her husband had feelings of insecurity. He lacked the control he had before. In the early stages of recovery, the addicted woman is overwhelmed with guilt, consequently continuing to allow others to control her behavior.

In addition to the marital problems, the children had more behavioral problems than previously realized. A woman under the influence is unable to see the broad picture of her children's behavior. Now that she functions better it is disconcerting to see them acting out, fighting with each other or disturbing outside systems. Naturally, she starts questioning her sobriety and wonders if her family and herself were in fact better off when she was actively using.

When Maggie stopped using, her first priority was to re-enter the family system in the role she believes she "should" have as mother, caretaker, nurturer. The children resented their mother's intrusion and defiantly resisted the change.

TREATMENT COMPONENTS

Family involvement in treatment is one of the most essential components in recovery. Recovering women have additional pressure put on them during this process, because in most cases they do not have a supportive spouse. When their male counterparts are recovering, in many cases, the entire family becomes involved in treatment willingly. Women continue to be looked upon negatively simply because they are chemically dependent. Husbands are resistant to treatment and also resist a commitment to a healthy relationship. Often men make the overall decision regarding the children and refuse to have them involved in their mother's treatment. The best outcome in treating a chemically dependent woman occurs when the entire family is involved.

COMPONENTS SUPPORTING TREATMENT

Additionally, significant components to support recovery in addicted women are child care; homogeneous groups; and alternative financial considerations. None of these components are critical when designing programs to be used most often by men.

Childcare arrangements are of primary concern if the program is designed to attract women. The logistic reality of doing this is challenging. Outpatient settings can more easily accommodate limited child care needs on premises while intensive programs and residential settings may support the patient with active coordination and advocacy efforts with appropriate attentive care givers.

Women have shown a greater degree of positive response and longer periods of abstinence when their treatment has included some sex therapy groups. As drinking and drugging patterns are more solitary, healthy relationships with friends and extended family are rarely available. The group will then take on this function.

Women have less money then men in our society today. Sliding scales and charity care are no more available to them than they are to men. Beyond that women do not always have access to family income, other financial information, insurance cards etc., and accessing this requires the assertiveness and ingenuity sometimes difficult for full functioning women. Delayed payments and a case worker to facilitate these financial systems is necessary.

CONCLUSION

Providers contend that women with families are not getting to treatment early on in the traditional outpatient addiction treatment community. Outpatient mental health data reveals that women are over represented at mental health facilities. We can assume from this that women perceive their needs to be met more often at a medical or psychiatrically oriented treatment experience. Families are more comfortable in accepting mental illness in one of their members, rather than chemical dependency. Our inference from this is that chemically dependent women perceive some safety in these treatment experiences and receive some nurturing. They may not perceive this to be the case in the addiction treatment community where responsibility for recovery is placed on the individual. The distinction between support and enabling are distorted to addicted women and their family. When this is looked at in the context of a woman's role, and coupled with feeling over burdened, it is easy to see how they arrive at this conclusion. The professional addiction community must, in addition to their primary focus on abstinence first respond with greater sensitivity that results in required family involvement, specialized groups, support services, and financial considerations. Treatment for women must include therapy for resolutions of the problems of intimacy, over responsibility, sexual and physical abuse, low sense of self esteem and of being incomplete without a relationship. In addition, providers must outreach to women more actively. The perception of addiction treatment being primarily for men needs to be overcome by clearly stating treatment goals and the availability of support services.

REFERENCES

Beckman, L., & Amaro, H. (1986). Personal and social difficulties faced by women and men entering alcoholism treatment. *Journal of Studies on Alcohol*, 47, 135-45.

Bourne, P.G., & Light, E. (1979). Alcohol problems in blacks and women. In J.H. Mendelson & N.K. Mello (Eds.), *The diagnosis and treatment of alcoholism* (pp. 84-123). New York: McGraw-Hill.

Corrigan, E. (1985). Gender differences in alcohol and other drug use. *Addictive Behavior*, 10, 314-17.

Herrington, R., Jacobson, G., & Benger, D. (1987). *Alcohol and drug abuse handbook*. Missouri: Warren H. Green Inc.

McGill, D., & Pearce, J.K. (1982). British families. In M. McGoldrick, J.K. Pearce, & J. Giordano (Eds.), *Ethnicity & family therapy*. (pp. 457-482). New York: Guilford Press.

McGuire, P.C. (1975). *The liberated woman*. Minnesota: Hazeldon Foundation.

Sandmaier, M. (1980). *The invisible alcoholics: Women and alcohol abuse in America*. New York: McGraw-Hill.

Stafford, R.A., & Pitway, J.M. (1977). Stigmatization of men and women problem drinking and their spouses: Differential perception and leveling of sex differences. *Journal of Studies on Alcohol, 38*, 2109-2121.

Family Treatment
with Chemically Dependent Gay Men
and Lesbians

Michael Shernoff, CSW, ACSW
Dana Finnegan, PhD, CAC

SUMMARY. This article will examine three issues: (1) the context within which family treatment of chemically dependent gay men and lesbians takes place; (2) the concepts which underlie any understanding of how to provide quality treatment to them; and (3) examples of practical approaches to providing such treatment.

INTRODUCTION

When chemical dependency counselors work with lesbians and gay men, it is important for them to consider both the context of their clients' lives and the concepts that influence them. First, as is true of all people struggling to recover from chemical dependency, the situations, feelings and attitudes that gay and lesbian people must deal with are often complex. Counselors need, however, to learn about, become sensitive to, acknowledge, and respond to the stressors specific to being lesbian or gay in this society.

Many of the difficulties experienced by lesbians or gay men that are unique to this population are generated by homophobia. For example, growing up as a gay man or lesbian in a heterosexual and

Michael Shernoff is founder and co-director of Chelsea Psychotherapy Associates in Manhattan. He is also a board member of the National Lesbian/Gay Health Foundation. Correspondence may be sent to Suite 1305, 80 Eighth Avenue, New York, NY 10011. Dana Finnegan is Co-Director of Discovery Counseling Center and is on the Board of the National Association of Lesbian and Gay Alcoholism Professionals. Correspondence may be sent to 271 Essex St., Millburn, NJ 07041.

121

homophobic family and having to keep secret one's sexual identity and affectional preference creates a powerful dysfunction that is a result not of the individual's homosexuality but of society's homophobia.

Thus it is not enough to say that clients' chemical dependency is always the only justifiable focus early in treatment. There are times when people's concerns about their sexual orientation may demand attention if they are to get or stay clean and sober. For instance, counselors need to recognize that sometimes it is very important to validate client's bitter or pained assertions that homophobia has seriously contributed to their chemical dependency.

Second, the definitions of family are changing in this culture, and the meanings of these new definitions need to be applied to lesbian's and gay men's lives. All too often there is a tendency to see lesbians and gay men primarily, if not solely, as individuals rather than as members of families of origin and as creators of new family systems. These families of creation may serve as additions to and/or replacements for nuclear families.

Therefore, a new comprehensive perspective on family is called for. Counselors need to know that gay men and lesbians may have children from earlier heterosexual relationships or may choose to have children by artificial insemination or through adoption. Furthermore, gay people who do not have children usually create a family system comprised of friends, some of whom may be current or ex-lovers.

CHEMICAL DEPENDENCY IS A FAMILY ILLNESS FOR ALL CLIENTS

In the 1970's, many chemical dependency counselors did not tend to "think family" when they worked with their chemically dependent client. If they thought about the family, it usually was to consider whether or not the spouse (usually the wife) could or would be helpful to the addicted client's recovery. But most counselors were not trained to think of the individual client as part of a larger system that impacted upon the client's efforts to recover from alcoholism or other drug abuse. That perspective has changed significantly in the past ten or fifteen years. Most professionals now treat chemical dependency as a family illness — at least with clients who are heterosexual or presumed to be so.

Unfortunately, this family perspective often does not get applied to clients who are lesbian or gay. All too frequently, counselors view and treat lesbian or gay clients as if they were single, discrete beings who hail from some distant and unknown planet without any human relationships. Counselors who do not assess lesbian or gay clients within the context of their families and friendships may provide these clients with good *individual* treatment, but too often ignore their larger, critically important human systems.

Perhaps because so many heterosexual counselors have little if any knowledge of or personal acquaintance with gay men or lesbians, they regard the lesbian or gay client as different and foreign to their experience. Thus, all too often, clinicians who know that a family perspective is vital to good treatment because chemical dependency is a *family* disease do not recognize the relevance of that perspective to gay men and lesbians who are chemically dependent.

THE DYSFUNCTIONAL NATURE OF HOMOPHOBIC FAMILIES

The third consideration counselors need to bear in mind is that growing up lesbian or gay in a "heterosexual family" is, by its very nature, a dysfunctional process — unless the family is not homophobic. Unfortunately, most families are at least somewhat homophobic. We are *not* saying that being lesbian or gay is dysfunctional. Rather, we are contending that when people grow up in a family system where they cannot be or say who they truly are, they are placed in a position of dysfunction. The prejudicial and oppressive values of the system and the actions based on those values make the *system*, not the individual, dysfunctional.

A system is dysfunctional when it forces its members to create a "false self" in order to survive. And that is precisely what children or adolescents who become aware of same-sex feelings and attractions do to survive. They create a false self which is different from who they really are and which prevents them from being known by even those closest to them. They must "split off" and hide a central part of themselves and must live a lie within the heart of their family. If other dysfunctional features exist in the family system – for example, chemical dependency – then the lesbian or gay child must contend with intensified problems, a kind of "double trouble."

This context and these concepts need to form the backdrop for all considerations about treatment approaches. Otherwise, we will add to our lesbian and gay male clients' problems, rather than contribute to their solutions.

Clinical Applications

Rhonda was a thirty five year old married housewife living in a medium sized midwestern city who had three prior admissions for detox. Each of her relapses had occurred while she was attending AA and ostensibly "working her program." She presented as seriously depressed and freely talked about wanting to hurt herself. During an individual counseling session, Doris, a lesbian nurse on the inpatient unit, shared with Rhonda that ten years earlier she had almost killed herself with prescription drugs and alcohol when this appeared to be an easier solution than leaving her husband of twelve years because she could no longer pretend that she was not attracted to women. Rhonda's eyes widened and she began to ask the nurse questions about her experience, without once ever admitting that she might have similar feelings. A few weeks after Rhonda was discharged Doris ran into Rhonda at an AA meeting. Rhonda told Doris that her disclosure provided for the first time in her adult life hope that perhaps she could stop using.

When questioned about why she had chosen to take this therapeutic approach, Doris explained that she had considered all other possible reasons for Rhonda's continued relapsing. As far as she could see there were no valid explanations for Rhonda's inability to maintain her sobriety when she was apparently doing everything right and going to AA every day. "I asked myself what could possibly be going on for this woman that I didn't know about or hadn't asked about that would explain her picking up. Something in the kind of pain that Rhonda was expressing reminded me of my own pain and conflict before I got sober," Doris said. "So I decided to take a chance by sharing my story with this patient. She was too fragile for me to ask directly about the possibility that she might be lesbian.''

Chemical dependency workers can learn an important lesson from this case. The lesson is that when a patient is relapsing into active drug/alcohol use without any obvious or apparently understandable reason, unresolved sexual identity conflict may well be the cause. Counselors need to be willing and ready to explore this possibility with appropriate patients.

One suggested intervention is to share Doris's story with a client and say "I don't know if this has any relevance for you, but I thought I would just share this anyway.'' When questioned about what in addition to her own intuition and the seeming lack of any reasons for Rhonda's inability to remain sober had clued Doris in to issues about lesbianism, Doris said she remembered that when she asked about Rhonda's marriage and sex life with her husband, Rhonda had ever so slightly shuddered and looked away. She denied any sexual or other abuse from her husband who was a non-drinker in Al-Anon. "This subtle reaction, that Rhonda was probably not even aware of, just rang a bell,'' Doris explained. Retelling Rhonda's story would be an excellent use of metaphor during treatment, a well-accepted family and systems technique.

Rhonda's case is a good illustration of why counselors need to question all clients about sexual orientation. It is the responsibility of each counselor to take the lead in this area the same way counselors routinely question early family history, dynamics of shame, denial and spirituality. By omitting questions about sexual orientation, or the more subtle questions about sexual or affectional feelings or fantasies for a person of the same sex, the counselor is not obtaining information about *all* the possible contributing factors for achieving and maintaining sobriety.

Thus during interviews or counseling sessions counselors should specifically and routinely be asking all clients questions about significant love relationships or spouses and lovers instead of *only* using the words marriages, husbands and wives. However, directly asking a patient who is only a few days sober, "What is your sexual orientation?'' may be too threatening for the client to answer honestly. A gentler way of opening this area up is to ask, "Have you ever had erotic or romantic feelings, fantasies or dreams that involved a person of the same sex *even if you have never acted on these feelings?"* Even if the client doesn't answer these kinds of questions and appears uncomfortable, counselors shouldn't take this silence as an indication that questions or statements about sexual orientation are not on target. Furthermore, it is important for counselors to ask them in order to convey to a frightened patient that the counselor is willing to talk about and hear issues pertaining to sexual identity.

Yet if a client's denial about his or her own sexual orientation is life threatening, the way it clearly was in Rhonda's case, then this denial must gently and empathically be addressed. If Rhonda had not even heard that there was a professional who could articulate her intimate concerns, she probably would have continued to use or possibly would have killed herself. Generally these are patients who have had chronic slips for no apparent reason, or people who wind up in psychiatric units following an unexplainable suicide attempt. Very often these are heterosexually married individuals who appear to be the farthest thing from lesbian or gay. They often have children. For these people, finally having a health care or substance abuse professional help them to look at this part of themselves in a nonjudgmental manner may be the *only* road to recovery.

NONTRADITIONAL FAMILIES

A family or systems perspective that includes the varieties of diverse family types that increasingly more Americans have created for themselves is essential in the field of substance abuse even if the identified patient is definitely not lesbian or gay. The authors are familiar with a case where a young adult was in rehab. His mother is a lesbian who has lived with her woman lover for the past twelve years. The lover was and remains an important parental figure to this young man. Even after both women visited him during rehab, none of the staff ever asked who his mother's friend was or about the nature of this young man's relationship with this woman.

When this man was discharged from rehab, he went to live with these two women, one of whom is in recovery and the other a long time member of Al-Anon. Thus he went directly from rehab to live in a family system that the treatment facility knew nothing about.

This man had not even discussed with his counselor how stressful it was for him to be living with two lesbians, even though he really liked both of them. This man has tremendous conflicts that stem from his being ashamed that his mother is a lesbian. He never talked about this during rehab, and for a long time never shared this information either with his sponsor or during meetings. Had one of these women been an active alcoholic or drug addict his prospects for continued sobriety would have been even more threatened.

SHAME REGARDING LOVING SOMEONE WHO IS LESBIAN OR GAY

A related area that needs to be explored is asking heterosexual patients in treatment about siblings who might be lesbian or gay. One seventeen year old woman just entering rehab for the first time was very frightened about her older sister. She adored this sister who was a lesbian and feared this might mean that she was one also. In addition, she was very ashamed that her beloved sister was a lesbian, and that if her friends found this out, they would tease her. If this young woman's counselors in the rehab had not asked about her family members in enough detail so that her sister's lesbianism was unmentioned, they could not have helped her deal either with her fears regarding her own sexual orientation or her shame about her sister. If either of these issues were left undiscussed in the early phase of recovery, they could have contributed to this person's relapse.

If parents have had a difficult time accepting the homosexuality of the brother or sister of the individual in treatment, or if this is a shame-filled family secret, probing this can offer valuable insights into how rigid and/or dysfunctional the family system is. This information is essential for the counselor to learn in order to ascertain what appropriate discharge and after-care planning will consist of.

ISOLATION

Long term treatment for the lesbian or gay man who is in recovery must take a family perspective which accounts for both his or her family of origin as well as any family systems that he or she has created. This is crucial because many lesbians and gay men grow up feeling terribly isolated. This sense of isolation persists and increases if they marry and have families. Even for some well-integrated lesbians or gay men who have friendship groups, lovers and perhaps even children, there often remain feelings of isolation and alienation that stem from unresolved feelings about their own homosexuality and society's homophobia.

As mentioned earlier, an important consideration counselors need to bear in mind is that growing up gay or lesbian in a family that assumes the heterosexuality of all its members is, by its very nature, a dysfunctional process — unless the family is not homophobic.

> Sam, always his grandmother's favorite, knew that he was attracted to other boys for most of his life, and somehow also knew that he couldn't talk about this with anyone. One day when he was ten, he was reading *Time* magazine with his grandmother. In response to a story about homosexuals she casually said, "We have to pray for those sick people." Sam recounted in a therapy session that he clearly remembers how much this comment frightened him and made him sad because he knew that grandma was talking about him but that she had no idea he was one of those people she was talking about. For the first time in his life he felt very distant from her since he now began to doubt whether she would love him if she knew that he was "one of those sick people."

For Sam this was the beginning of creating a false self that resulted in his having a dysfunctional relationship with an otherwise generally stable and loving family. His resolve to hide his strong feelings for other boys and men grew after this incident. Perceiving that in order to keep his family's adoration he needed to pretend to be different from who he really was caused Sam to develop a lot of shame about some of his most central and most normal feelings. In order to protect his status of being loved and valued by his family, he began trying to deny that he even had feelings for boys because his feelings were different from what was expected of him by his family. He also carefully avoided discussing these feelings and tried to behave in the manner that would assure the continued respect and love of his family. This was the beginning of Sam's behaving in a co-dependent manner that has plagued him ever since. Luckily, aside from normal unexamined homophobia and heterosexual bias, Sam's family was not dysfunctional in other ways. Thus there were not secrets related to alcoholism, violence or incest that also had to be hidden and would have become additional sources of shame or guilt.

Once again we reiterate that we are *not* saying that being lesbian or gay is in itself dysfunctional. Rather we are pointing out that society's prejudicial and oppressive values that simply assume that everyone is the same, i.e., heterosexual, result in the majority of children who grow up to be lesbian or gay feeling like outsiders within their own families. This feeling of difference becomes translated into being wrong or bad. If other dysfunctional features exist in the same family system — for example, alcoholism — then the gay or lesbian child must contend with intensified problems which compound the hurt they already feel living as a member of their particular family.

SHAME THAT PREDATES HOMOSEXUAL FEELINGS

As the authors do long term intra-psychic therapy, we are increasingly finding that even after many years abstinence from alcohol or drugs our clients discover memories of early childhood abuse and incest that have been buried deep in their unconscious. Very often the abuse or incest occurred even before the child knew that he was gay or she was lesbian. Most often the shame and sense of difference caused by the abuse predates any sense of sexual identity formation. During the course of therapy, most gay men or lesbians will easily recall early childhood memories of feeling different or bad which they connect to their homosexuality. While these memories and feelings are important to explore, the skilled therapist must also lead his or her client in a search that could turn up feelings of self-loathing and low self-esteem that occurred even before their feelings for persons of the same sex began to emerge. The counselor then can help the client differentiate between internalized homophobia and other sources of shame.

Especially with clients who are in recovery from substance abuse, questioning them about memories they have that predate the formation of a sexual identity is essential. Some people knew that they were attracted to other boys or girls from their earliest awareness. Other people did not begin to recognize these feelings or suppressed them until puberty or even adulthood. Often gay or lesbian clients will not have looked at their lives and experiences prior to their first feelings of shame or difference that stem from the onset of homosexual feelings. In order for true healing and insight to occur, clients must learn to differentiate between the problems that have their etiology in traumas experienced as a result of situations that were distinct and separate from their homosexuality. Yet the shame about their early homosexual feelings is usually viewed by clients as the only reason they have felt different or damaged. Skilled therapy needs to help clients tease apart these separate, yet interrelated issues. One manifestation of internalized homophobia is commonly exhibited when lesbian or gay clients blame all of their early painful feelings solely upon their homosexuality. A thorough therapeutic exploration of the early family reality is necessary for both the therapist and client to gain a good understanding of what it was like for this child to grow up, and in what ways he or she was damaged long before same sex feelings emerged.

HEALING THE CHEMICALLY DEPENDENT FAMILY SYSTEM

When a lesbian or gay man abuses alcohol or drugs, the dysfunction the substance abuse creates for his or her family of creation (lover, roommate or friends) is in addition to the historical dysfunction each lesbian or gay man grew up with as a member of a homophobic family. These dual aspects of dysfunctions occur simultaneously and inter-relatedly for both the person who is abusing as well as for his or her support system or lover, friends and nuclear family. For real and lasting sobriety to be achieved these different but complementary dysfunctions must be addressed and brought into the open for all parties involved.

A family or systems perspective is also useful working with lesbians or gay men who have a well integrated identity as gay or lesbian. One characteristic of men and women who have developed a positive lesbian or gay identity is that they have formed a strong family of supportive friends and perhaps are in a committed relationship. The following example illustrates how understanding the dynamics of these families can be useful when working with a gay man in recovery.

> Ralph is a fifty year old gay white man who lives in Manhattan. He has been with his lover Paul for fourteen years. He sought out therapy with one of the authors because he was concerned about his alcohol and cocaine use. After the first consultation he began to attend AA and recently celebrated his two year anniversary clean and dry.
>
> Ralph and Paul had always done a lot of cocaine together, especially when having sex. Even after Ralph entered the program, Paul continued to use in their home and would attempt to seduce Ralph into using so that they could have sex. On advice from his sponsor, Ralph elected to tell Paul that he would love to have sex with him, but only if he wasn't under the influence of any drug. This enraged Paul, and they have not had sex in over eighteen months.
>
> In Ralph's thirteenth month of sobriety, he and Paul had an argument that escalated into a fist fight. Greatly shaken by the domestic violence, Ralph temporarily moved out of their apartment and in with his sponsor. Simultaneously he began to attend Al-Anon meetings.
>
> They eventually negotiated Ralph's moving back in on the condition that Paul stop using drugs and go to AA. Newly sober, Paul was not interested in having sex. This caused Ralph a great deal of frustration since he and Paul shared the same bed, and they did not have any physical affection. Shortly after Paul celebrated 90 days sober Ralph and he began talking about slowly trying to resume being physical and sexual. Two days later Paul told Ralph that he had used cocaine recently.

Because the only blood family that Ralph has is one sister who lives over fifteen hundred miles away, and with whom he is not particularly close, Paul is his primary family. Their extended family of creation has shrunk since the onset of AIDS. More than ten close friends who they considered to be "family" have died in the past four years.

This couple is exceptionally stressed for several reasons. First of all they are mourning their decimated friendship group. Two of these people died in the past three months, and both Ralph and Paul were very involved in caring for these men as they got progressively more debilitated. Their relationship is currently and actively dysfunctional since Paul is still abusing cocaine. Ralph feels very dependent upon Paul even though due to Paul's drug abuse he is rarely emotionally available to Ralph. Only a family/systems approach to treatment can address the multiple stressors Ralph is currently struggling with. Ralph's treatment consists in part of encouraging him to build a new family within AA that includes his sponsor and supportive friends he has met in the rooms. The suggestion that Ralph actively pursue building a new family within AA was aimed at removing the pressure Paul felt about having to be all things to Ralph.

Using a family/systems approach to treatment helps the newly recovering lesbian or gay client to understand, value and nurture his or her relationships with lovers and friends as well as blood family. In effect this form of treatment is essential for lesbians and gay men who have proven themselves remarkably resourceful in creating new families that support and celebrate their lifestyle and relationships. For recovering people who are lucky enough to live in areas where there are lesbian and gay AA meetings, sober families of recovering people have been created as well, and are an essential component to living clean and sober.

THE IMPACT OF AIDS
ON GAY AND LESBIAN PEOPLE IN RECOVERY

Counselors and therapists need to recognize another important issue that is relevant to family work with their lesbian and gay clients. For more than ten years now, since the onset of the AIDS health crisis, these families have lost many members. Lesbians and gay men have taken care of beloved friends with AIDS and watched helplessly as they died.

For some people like Ralph and Paul, almost entire friendship groups have been wiped out. This has created some new problems for recovering people who have achieved and maintained their sobriety in lesbian and gay AA. People with AIDS share in these rooms about their illness, deterioration, fears and early demise. Others are sharing about their pain, rage and grief at having loved ones achieve sobriety, only to watch them wither and die from AIDS. Along with the joy and serenity of sobriety, the lesbian and gay AA rooms contain an enormous amount of pain and sadness these days. Some of our clients report that they cannot go to these meetings as much anymore, or in some cases at all, because it is too painful to listen to what is being shared, to see sober friends waste away, and to sit in the room with all the ghosts of friends who have died.

Gay or lesbian clients who are struggling to maintain sobriety today face the additional stress of living in a community increasingly devastated by AIDS. Their friends, their lovers or they themselves may be infected with HIV or may be dying from AIDS. Counselors must recognize that these friendship groups and relationships constitute families for their clients. In the counseling they must clearly communicate their understanding that these are families, and then validate and honor these family systems. Doing this will empower both the client and his or her family of creation. Only by fully empathizing with how powerful the connections are between the client and the person or people who are ill can the counselor help the client do the grief work and mourning that is necessary. Ultimately the client will need the counselor's help and support to build new relationships and family systems to replace the ones that have been decimated.

RECOMMENDATIONS

1. Assess clients' multiple family structures (families of origin and creation), the impact of chemical dependency on those structures, and the impact of those structures on the clients' chemical dependency.

2. Provide support to clients for distancing from homophobic families of origin, especially those who see the clients' chemical dependency as a "natural" component or outgrowth of the "sickness" of homosexuality.

3. Recognize and help clients see that families of creation and origin may need to keep them, the Identified Patient, actively chemically dependent in order to maintain the I.P.'s role as symptom bearer. Keeping the I.P. in this role can serve the function of helping families deny their own dysfunctions.

4. Provide support for distancing from chemically dependent families of creation (origin, also) when they view clients' chemical dependency as "natural" to the lesbian/gay lifestyle and not as a destructive illness.

5. Help lesbian and gay clients who may be newly "coming out" not to jump into new relationships in their first year of recovery.

6. Be aware of the issues facing newly recovering lesbian or gay people who are part of established couples. These clients need help in modifying their expectations and in finding or creating support networks.

7. Recognize and help clients recognize that the recovery process can stir up their internalized homophobia which they blunted or anesthetized with alcohol and/or drugs. Also, their recovery may stir up other people's homophobia as the recovering clients attempt to take their place in the family of origin as their authentic selves.

CONCLUSION

It is important for chemical dependency counselors to keep certain points in mind when working with gay or lesbian clients. One is that chemical dependency is a family disease, one that intimately and powerfully affects all who are involved in the family system of the chemically dependent person, regardless of his or her sexual orientation. This fact requires a family systems perspective if one is to adequately address the ravages of the disease. Another point is that very little support or recognition is afforded to lesbian or gay love relationships, friendships, and families.

Thus the well-meaning counselor who fails to work from a family perspective with lesbian and gay clients is not helping clients to establish the foundations of long-term recovery. Rather, this counselor may be undermining the recovery process by blocking or at the least ignoring the system within which clients must recover. It is imperative to know whether or not clients' support systems are positive or negative. Without this information, aftercare cannot be adequately planned or carried out. The last and most important point centers on counselors' attitudes. Unless counselors are willing to respect and honor the created families of lesbians and gay men and to work with those systems *as family systems*, the treatment offered will be seriously lacking, if not directly harmful.

REFERENCES

Finnegan, D.G., & McNally, E.B. (1987). *Dual identities: Counseling chemically dependent gay men and lesbians.* Center City, MN: Hazelden.

Finnegan, D.G., McNally, E.B., & Fischer, G. (1984). Alcoholism and chemical dependency. In F. Schwaber & M. Shernoff (Eds.), *Sourcebook on lesbian/gay issues* (pp. 47-49). New York: National Gay Health Education Foundation.

Finnegan, D.G., McNally, E.B. (1988). The lonely journey: Lesbians and gay men who are co-dependent. In M. Shernoff & W; A. Scott (Eds.), *The sourcebook on lesbian/gay health care* (2nd edition) (173-182). Washington, D.C.: The National Lesbian/Gay Health Foundation.

Hanley-Hackenbruck, P. (1989). Psychotherapy and the "coming out" process. *Journal of Gay & Lesbian Psychotherapy, 1*(1), 21-39.

Pohl, M. (1988). Recovery from alcoholism and chemical dependence for lesbians and gay men. In M. Shernoff & W.A. Scott (Eds.), *The sourcebook on lesbian/gay health care* (2nd ed.) (pp. 169-172). Washington, DC: National Lesbian and Gay Health Foundation.

Ratner, E. (1988). Treatment issues for chemically dependent lesbians and gay men. In M. Shernoff & W.A. Scott (Eds.), *The sourcebook on lesbian/gay health care* (2nd ed.) (pp. 162-168). Washington, DC: National Lesbian and Gay Health Foundation.

Schaefer, S., Evans, S., & Coleman, E. (1987). Sexual orientation concerns among chemically dependent individuals. *Journal of Chemical Dependency Treatment, 1*(1), 121-140.

Shernoff, M. (1984). Family therapy for lesbian and gay clients. *Social Work, 29*(4), 393-396.

Ziebold, T.O. & Mongeon, J. (Eds.) (1982). *Alcoholism & homosexuality.* New York: The Haworth Press, Inc.

Understanding Cultural Values of Latino Male Alcoholics and Their Families: A Culture Sensitive Model

Myriam Laureano, CSW, CAC
Edward Poliandro, PhD

SUMMARY. This article discusses the devastating impact that problem drinking and alcoholism have on immigrant Latinos and their families. A parallel process of the progression of deteriorating cultural values due to immigrational stressors and alcoholism is identified. This process continues as clinicians treat two and three generations of alcohol/drug addiction and co-dependency. A culturally Sensitive Assessment Model that can be integrated in the treatment of individuals, families and groups is also developed. A case example is discussed.

INTRODUCTION

Ethnicity and culture play a critical role in the development of individual identity. Yet until fairly recently little work had been done to define how these elements are integrated into alcoholism treatment models. We now know more than ever about human life and human struggles, the cycles that enrich or deplete individual and family functioning and about illness as a process. Yet most people who come for treatment are still evaluated without regard to

Myriam Laureano is a member of the Training and Education Committee of the Alcoholism Council of Greater New York and maintains a private psychotherapy practice. Edward Poliandro is on the faculty of the Mount Sinai School of Medicine and Account Executive for Human Affaires International in New York. He maintains a private psychotherapy and management consulting practice.

the primary framework on which their identity is based and their behavior understood: their ethnicity and culture. Just as the addiction process itself has a life-long impact on the individual's sense of self, so too their ethnicity and culture form an enduring core in their personality.

Like other ethnic groups in the United States, today's urban population of Latino immigrants must cope with a myriad of conflicts: the mix of generations, traditions, religions, social roles and social status, economic shifts, language differences and socio-political marginalization. Many resort to alcohol or drug use when the pressures become intolerable and hopes diminish. If addressed without regard to the ethnicity and culture of origin, the Latino alcoholic can once again feel marginalized and alienated by the host culture and reject treatment. De La Cancela (1986) warns about the potential for stereotyping that can be interpreted from making generalizations about behavior in any culture. With this in mind the authors acknowledge that cultural values discussed here are presented in the context of not only the reality of our varied multicultural society (as it is in New York City) but also the transitional values and roles of the host culture as well as our own. The following paper outlines the key concepts of Latino culture and the relationship of the immigration experience with patterns of drinking. From this framework a Culture Sensitive Assessment Model is developed that clinicians can use to integrate relative value systems into the treatment of alcoholics and their families.[1]

PART I: KEY CONCEPTS IN LATINO CULTURE

Dignidad

In the Latino culture, a person's dignity encompasses the whole self. This includes self-esteem and self-worth. The sense of self-worth is measured by *who* one is, not *what* one owns. Self-worth also relates to attachment to family, extended family, community and country. A sense of individuality is related to good social judgement, appropriate public and private conduct, and security in the roles of man, woman, father, mother, family member and worker. A sense of pride in the ability to uphold one's dignity is also admired as a virtue. *Verguenza* or shame is viewed as a virtue in relationship to dignity. *No tener verguenza* or not to have shame means that a person has behaved in a culturally unacceptable way and has trespassed cultural boundaries.

Respeto

The value of *respeto* binds and defines the family system. Self respect means to respect oneself and to respect others. The lack of respect or *"una falta de respeto"* really means a *fault* in respect. It is viewed not as a situational mistake, but a character defect. *Respeto* is closely linked to *dignidad*. When a person is lacking in respect, his/her dignity as a person is also questioned. Children are taught at a very early age that all behavior and boundary definition stems from respect. When parents say *"respeta eso"* (respect this) they mean "do not touch that." *"Tu no tienes respeto"* (you have no respect) is a disciplinary term used to discourage inappropriate behavior regardless of its seriousness. A child's lack of respect for an object implies disrespect to the parents. The parent's non-verbal and verbal signals, and body language must be respected and obeyed equally.

The value of respect extends beyond the family to the larger community. The culture permits a parent to discipline other children in the community. Children are expected to listen to all adults as authority figures. Thus *respeto* extends to property, group conduct, and public and private gatherings.

Confianza

"Dar confianza" – to give trust or *"tener confianza"* – to be trusting are ways showing respect for oneself as well as for others. But trusting precipitously implies a lack of good judgement. A person can ask permission to be granted more *confianza* in a relationship. This may be considered suspicious and although granted, the trust is still in question. *"Perder confianza"* or to lose trust is serious because so much of the *dignidad* value is tied in with respect. *Cojer confianza* is to cross a boundary without permission. *Palabra de honor* or word of honor is used to demonstrate trust in terms of establishing boundaries in relationships.

Personalismo

This refers to face-to-face contact with primary relations and with institutions. For example, Latinos/as prefer to do business in person. Participation in groups depends more on the strength of ties to individual group members rather than on ties to an abstract cause. "Family style" communication is the norm and often precedes and introduces business.

Hospitalidad

Hospitality builds trust and develops relationships. No matter how casual or brief the encounter, a host-guest relationship is expected: the offering of beverages, a seat or help. Making people feel comfortable — mentally and physically — shows "*una buena educacion.*" A person may have various academic degrees as part of formal education, but if he/she is lacking in hospitality, the family's ability to educate and articulate appropriate manners and conduct is seriously questioned.

Individualismo

Parents recognize a child's individuality from infancy. A child's physical resemblance to the family constitutes membership in that family. However, his/her intrinsic sense of self is seen as God-given, e.g., *salio como Dios lo hizo* or he/she came out as God made him. Each child is seen as unique and having the right to develop that uniqueness within the cultural values of respect, dignity and trust.

Sex role differentiation, another aspect of individuation begins at birth. Children are taught to play together, but mostly boys with boys and girls with girls. Character development is focused on self respect, humility and appropriate conduct. The ability to control the aggressive instincts is highly valued. Parents view children as good when they demonstrate a spirit of cooperation and place families' interest before individual needs. Moving away from one's family of origin is a gradual process which requires the family's spoken or unspoken approval.

Inclan (1989) points out the difference of a modern industrial society as an agricultural economy as Puerto Rico was in the 1960's and other Latino countries still are. The adolescent or young adult is engaged in an apprenticeship role which serves the labor demands of an agrarian economic system. They are expected to stay and work for the family's well-being. First generation parents may still have these values and think that children are children until they demonstrate adult behaviors, such as forming a new family and acquiring a good job. In addition parents may tend to return to a more traditional sex role expectation for girls than for boys.

Machismo — refers to behaviors, attitudes and societal expectations that shape male identity in terms of social image and social role as *un hombre completo* (a complete man). The psycho-dynamic and developmental approaches to understanding the impact of machismo on male identity would be incomplete and possibly erroneous if not understood within a larger cultural and socio-economic framework. De La Cancela (1986) emphasizes posits that machismo has multidimensional meanings which encompass different societies with patriarchal roots and which can only be understood by appreciating its socio-historical, political and economic determinants.

PART II: ALCOHOL USE
AND THE MIGRATION EXPERIENCE
AMONG LATINO FAMILIES

Since the early 1900's and especially after World War II, Puerto Rican families have migrated to the United States in search of jobs, education, political refuge and adventure. As in other migrations throughout history, the new arrivals tended to internalize the tensions that surfaced between themselves and their host culture. Racism and poverty compounded Latinos/as' struggle with isolation and ethnic identity. While racism exists in Puerto Rico and other Latino countries — most often through a combination of race, color and class factors — the racism these Latino groups encountered in the immigration experience caused a profound and devastating effect on their sense of self (Mizio, 1974). For example, Puerto Ricans who were traditionally accustomed to a wider range of color identification now had to accept the racial standard of the host culture which defines individuals as White or non-White. Rodriquez notes:

> This host culture definition has had a profoundly negative effect on Puerto Rican's self-concept as well as being a major determinant of the socio-economic future of the next generation. . . . Two facts about the racial order were quite clear. One was that the context into which Puerto Ricans stepped offered only two paths — one to the White world and one to the non-White world. Choice of path was dependent on racial classification according to United States standards. Use of these standards divided the group, negated the cultural existence of Puerto Ricans, and ignored their expectations that they be treated irrespective of race, as a culturally intact group . . . " (1989:56)

These two paths presented serious consequences for immigrating families. On one hand, the attempt to fully acculturate with the host culture and superimpose an "instant identity" often meant rejecting the values of the homeland culture, and the sense of self that comes from membership in one's community. Mizio notes the price the Latino has paid is "denial of self and heritage and a sacrifice of personal integrity. Whether society permits him a self-definition of white or black, he is faced with an identity problem" (1974:79). On the other hand, enclosing oneself in one's immigrational community in an effort to protect against hostility experienced from the host culture and secure support from traditional values has often led to collective isolation and marginalization. The alternatives in dealing with acculturation place Latinos/as at high risk for problem drinking, as alcohol is an integral part of all social activities. For the Latino/a who has relinquished most if not all ties to the mother culture, drinking may become a way of dealing with the loss and sense of betrayal. In similar fashion when the choice is to maintain cultural identity through primary ties with the immigrational community, drinking can move from a social ritual bonding people together, to a way of dealing with dissolution of hopes and dreams of succeeding in the new world.

Role Conflict and Alcohol Consumption

Once an immigrant family begins to interact with the host community, value conflicts emerge. This often occurs when Latino families begin to access social services, health care and school systems. The value of the extended family and *compadrazo* (kinship through godparent roles) has often been misunderstood by social service and health care systems. The impact of these cultural misunderstandings are often internalized and negatively affect the families sense of self and their sex roles. For example the male may experience a loss of respeto and dignidad as he perceives these systems unresponsive to assisting him in his primary role of protecting and providing for his family. Women experience the loss of their traditional role as they now have to take a more aggressive stance to negotiate the host cultures system which they often experience as hostile and alienating.

As these increasing role conflicts exacerbate a breakdown in the "traditional" sense of self the need becomes greater to socialize with one's own. In the Latino culture, drinking is a man's way of socializing with other males in the community. Men often play cards or dominoes outdoors or in front of the *bodega* (grocery store); this often evokes the feeling of being back in Puerto Rico. They bond by talking in Spanish about the "old country," and by sharing the pain of culture shock and the stress of acculturation. Alcohol is the preferred substance because Puerto Ricans traditionally toast national pride with rum. During early stages of assimilation, some women also began to drink beer with their husbands' permission at a party or on a special occasion. This drinking behavior was never welcomed by the Anglo culture that was uncomfortable with this outdoor display of routine socializing. Many Puerto Rican men, feeling ridiculed and marginalized began to take their drinking indoors. They developed social clubs, usually named after a town back home. These clubs served many functions: support, entertainment, sharing of resources and planning social events. Heavy drinking was no longer reserved for weekends only. As their experience of unemployment grew, so did the importance of these clubs as places to "hang out" outside the home. When material gains seemed beyond reach and upward-mobility an aspiration so highly valued by the dominant culture so unattainable, the value of *la dignidad* (a belief in the innate worth and inner importance of each individual) could be re-enforced through these socializing activities. *El respeto* (respect) was critical especially when the men were experiencing neither respect or even acknowledgement from the host culture.

The growing generation gap between immigrant parents and their bi-cultural children has been another source of constant conflict for the whole family. However, it has been more difficult for men to find jobs than for women. Being without a job is often experienced as a loss of identity, and the positive aspects of machismo. Losing one's job can be equated to losing one's position in the family as *el jefe de la casa*, or the head of the household. This drastic shift in roles and loss of social status has often resulted in escape drinking to help men release tensions and deal with the loss of their manhood and their position in their families. Feelings of isolation and low self-worth brought on by unemployment and social marginalization aggravated the drinking. They could not communicate these feelings to their boss, their wife, or the sons and daughters who were now becoming bi-cultural. The earlier support group of drinking buddies turned from reminiscing about traditional "good" values to blaming themselves and seeing themselves as failures. Children assuming bi-cultural values were beginning to lose respect for these fathers. Furthermore, the woman who once tolerated the man's drinking now criticizes his staying out with his friends and accuses him of irresponsibility.

The Impact of Alcoholism on the Family

As the Latino family adapted to the new stressor of problem drinking, traditional values deteriorated. When men lose their jobs, the family most often is forced to seek public assistance. In order to cope, the more previously open system of the extended family becomes a closed system which fears loss of primary support and more humiliation. A women fears she is losing her husband to alcohol and to his street friends and losing her children to the streets or to the Child Welfare system for neglect. This pressure leads her to use the health care system for herself. First she may be prescribed tranquilizers and later other medications to alleviate all her somatic symptoms. She may ask some of her female friends to share their medications for other related physical symptoms. For example, Puerto Rican women customarily share these drugs among themselves to combat *"mal de los nervios,"* a state of nervousness or anxiousness that is often described among Puerto Ricans and other Latinos (Aguirre-Molina, 1990). As attention is being paid to the mother's using medications to alleviate her emotional and somatic complaints, or to her childrens' behavior or school problems, the relationship of the father's loss of status in the family and resulting increased drinking often goes unrecognized. The woman may then begin to feel she is losing her ability to keep the family together. Her children become partners in the effort to prevent total collapse. The perfect partner may be the oldest son as he fits the cultural prescription of the role. *Parentified child.*

These role reversals constitute the beginning signals of a dysfunctional family system. In this system the woman as wife/mother often becomes co-dependent and a possible addict herself. In her work on co-dependency, Wilson-Scharf states that " . . . co-dependents frequently become ill from attempting to control the uncontrollable" (1986:54). This need to control increases their need for caretaking — doing for others which is often manifested as an exaggerated effort to put the family's needs first, while abandoning her own needs.

The feelings of economic uncertainty, ungrieved loss of manhood plus the mother's demand that the children enlist as partners in managing the family's survival, often drives Latino adolescents to seek role models in the streets. Historically, with the "street acculturation" came a subculture of dissatisfied youth who looked to drugs — marijuana, heroin, hallucinogenics — as the answer to feelings of alienation and hopelessness. But the families experienced an even more devastating deterioration. As the drug subculture forces many adolescents into illegal behaviors, the men drinking at the corner feel ashamed of being their fathers. By the 1980's, Puerto Ricans migrating to the mainland, saw a generation of children who have dropped out of school in the 8th grade, talk back to their parents, steal money from the house and community businesses, and disgrace the family with unwanted pregnancies and police arrests.

Respect for authority figures and value of trust deteriorated. Where once adults could reprimand their children for inappropriate behaviors, now all the rules have been broken and no one feels good enough to stand to be a role model. The drug epidemic advanced while parents' alcoholism and co-dependence continued unabated.

Despite this deterioration of the family values, the co-dependent wife usually remains loyal to the family. She uses her physical somatic complaints—which could become severe illnesses and addiction—to draw the family back to the nest. The loss of trust and an increasing sense of discouragement with the family may lead her to reach out in crisis to the priest or pastor and later or simultaneously to the local *espiritista* (a channel or guide to the spirit world). She reaches out to these resources in an attempt and hope that her husband and children will follow. If these numerous attempts at helping her family fail, she then begins to feel unworthy and may withdraw and use alcohol and prescribed drugs. Her rigidity and lack of consistency make her feel fragmented and out of control with her family. Her authority over her children becomes increasingly compromised as her behavior become less consistent. During these times, she also may becomes more vulnerable to the criticisms of more traditional members of the family, especially her mother.

PART III:
A CULTURE-SENSITIVE ASSESSMENT MODEL

Research indicates that minorities tend to get more frequently misdiagnosed compared to the rest of the population. Studies also show that lower social classes are diagnosed with more severe psychiatric disorders than middle-class people (Inclan, 1989). Latinos/as have encountered similar experiences in seeking help for chemical dependency. Treatment approaches found to be most effective for chemical dependency have included a combination of cognitive, client-centered reality based, family systems and The 12-Step Model approaches. However Latino groups have not received the benefits of the inroads made in developing treatment for chemical dependency, as the assessment and diagnostic tools have not integrated a culture-sensitive structure as part of service delivery. Rivera-Ramos' work on the effectiveness of adapting mental health models to individuals living in Puerto Rico is an example of what happens when cultural and socio-political factors are only acknowledged but not integrated into the evaluation and treatment process. She notes that "if these models do not result in losing clients they help in "curing" them of their cultural values and the clinician is not acting as a therapist but as an agent of transculturation" (trans., 1984:5).

The Culture Sensitive Assessment Model encompasses the Inclan's seminal work on the relationship between the Latino migrational experience and the deterioration of cultural values (1985). The model presented below introduces the role of alcoholism and the immigrational experience as viewed as both contributing to cultural value deterioration, as well as being an unsuccessful attempt to cope with loss of cultural identity.

The 12-Step Model also provides the structure and philosophy into which, this Culture Sensitive Model can be integrated, as it deals with the core of self-hood, which can be seen as culturally determined. The 12-Step Model also promotes a self-inventory of past identities and experiences in an effort to establish a new "sober identity."

A. Clinical Objectives
of a Culture-Sensitive Assessment Model

Cultural values provide an individual with a sense of self and membership in a community. A Culture-Sensitive Assessment Model offers clinicians the framework within which to understand the treatment of chemical dependency. This model is comprised of the following objectives:

1. It views the behaviors and lives of individual families on a continuum of socio-cultural adaptation.

2. It allows the clinician to engage the individual/family in understanding their current status on this continuum and how alcohol and drug abuse have affected their beliefs and values. In the recovery phase of treatment this model provides the opportunity to integrate new sober values in clients' belief systems and/or acculturation process.

3. It decreases fear and shame of negative stereotypical percep-

tions, while increasing the family's ability to trust and invite the professional into their world.

4. It allows both clinician and client to dynamically participate in a reciprocal cultural educational interaction whereby both can cross-over to each other's cultures.

B. Steps and Guidelines to Integrating a Culture-Sensitive Assessment Model

The interview begins with a greeting of welcome. Shaking hands with everyone in a Latino family is a much more accepted social behavior than with other ethnic groups. Next follows an exploration of the family's main reason for the consultation. The clients may refer first to concrete problems (e.g., job loss, school problems, etc.) and leave out issues of drug/alcohol use. If the clinician is working out of a drug or alcohol-specific agency, first he/she introduces its admission criteria. The clinician's own role can be introduced as part of the intake design to learn about the family's cultural values, a way of introducing the concept of mutual education. Immigrational information and related issues provide a good starting point, after the basic questions about place and length of their current residency. The following are sample questions and approaches that may be used in engaging the client/family.

1. "What types of problems did you and your family deal with when you came to the States?" Here the family can be complimented for their achievements and for surviving their failures and continuing to grow. After this acknowledgement, questions about drinking and drug use can be explored.

2. "How did members of your family relax at the end of a hard working or hard struggling week? I understand that music, dancing and drinking is a part of your culture. Do you make or have time for fun? Was it different back home?" These questions will give the interviewer a sense of the family perception of alcohol and drinking in general. If they reveal a drinking problem, the clinician can start with a few informational questions, being careful not to confront it before building more trust through this cultural process. If they do not respond to the drinking at all, the concept of losing control can be introduced as follows. "In the Latino culture a man is allowed to

drink but not lose control. What do you think?'' If there is a defensive reaction to this question, the family's cultural beliefs and values can continue to be explored.

3. ''In my experience in working with Latinos/as, I have learned of the differences that exist between various groups such as Cubans and Puerto Ricans, for example. I have also noticed differences between American culture and Latino culture. We can spend part of this session for me to learn more about your culture and for me to clarify questions you may have about American values.'' The clinician may use an example of a time when he/she felt misunderstood by a Latino/a client and later learned the cultural value that made the difference in the erroneous interpretation. This can apply whether the worker is Anglo or Latino and representative of cross-cultural interaction. It is also important to stress how North American family values are changing and to communicate to Latino families that all ethnic groups including Anglos, are struggling with changing social roles and expectations.

4. To explore the family's level of acculturation, questions may be asked about how the family learned English and how this process of learning influences their behavior. ''When you first came to the States, how did the family learn English? Who learned English first? How did you feel when your children learned English with greater ease?'' The answer to these questions may reveal the conflicts in the family's experience of acculturation, as well as the children's experience of the differences between home and school or street and how role reversal may have occurred when they are called to interpret on their parents' behalf.

5. To explore relationship dynamics within the nuclear and the extended family, clinicians may ask: ''Who lives with the family?'' This may provide information about support systems and how the boundaries are established. Latinos/as expect certain behaviors or unspoken rules to outline the boundaries. For example, a source of cultural conflict for immigrant families is the on-going relationships with grandparents and other family members. If these relatives come to live with the family, the boundaries of the nuclear family begin to shift or change. This often causes painful imbalances because the family is already stressed by the adjustment demands of the new culture.

6. "How has it been to deal with various systems like school, housing, work, health care, social services, church? How have these systems responded to your family's needs as compared to similar systems in your country?" These questions may provide information about the degree to which the family experiences itself as part of the new community, or being marginalized and alienated from it. Isolation or integration from the rest of the community can lead to conflict, race confusion, and ultimately deterioration of family structure. All of the above are high risk indicators for chemical dependency and a co-dependent closed family system.

7. As in most cultures, families find it difficult to openly discuss concerns about sex. Latinos often feel more comfortable expressing their feelings by talking about physical symptoms. Therefore questions about health and illness may provide an opening to explore attitudes and fears about such issues as sexual functioning (including heterosexuality, bisexuality, homosexuality and Lesbianism), birth control practices, and sexually transmitted diseases. With the spread of AIDS in the Latino community, this becomes an even more crucial area for clinicians to explore as judgement in their chemically-dependent clients is manifested in memory lapses and out of control behavior. In addition their co-dependent partners are also at high risk for HIV infection, as they are usually not the focus of AIDS education. They become vulnerable to the wishes of a seductive partner as they are unable to say "NO" – a primary symptom of co-dependency – for fear of rejection and abandonment. Latinos/as may feel insulted and consider these questions *una falta de respeto* (a lack of respect) or as an overstepping of the trust boundary (*cojer confianza*). To assure a cultural acceptance it is advisable to ease into these sensitive areas with statements such as *"perdonen ustedes, quiero pedir permiso para hacer unas preguntas que a veces podran parecer muy personales pero son necesarias para poderles servir mejor"* (Excuse me, I would like to ask permission to ask some questions that sometimes might seem too personal but that are necessary so I can serve you better).

8. All cultures utilize ritual to provide a deeper understanding of the "meaning of life." In Latino/a cultures spirituality often include rituals including Catholicism, *espiritismo, santerisimo*, and *curanderismo*. Questions like "Does the family practice a particular religion? Does your family use any other religious practices for

help with problems such as drinking" can yield information about the family's relationship to religious practices as well as traditional treatment approaches.

9. Television, radio and news media have a highly influential impact on the cultural values of people. Asking families about the effects of television on their children can raise parental awareness while exploring the rate of acculturation in a family. Does the family watch more Spanish speaking programs than English speaking or both? In response to these questions families begin to highlight the differences between cultures and the possible loss of traditional values. Focusing on stereotypic expectations of success for men and women, may increase this sense of inadequacy and fatality in living up to host cultural gender role expectations as well as their own. This may provide a bridge for the clinician to further explore what role alcohol plays in dealing with feelings of inadequacy and shattered role expectations.

PART IV: CASE ILLUSTRATION

The following two excerpts from early initial interviews illustrate how clinicians can integrate a cultural framework into their work with Latino/a alcoholics and their families. The authors have specially chosen two families from a Puerto Rican and Cuban background to demonstrate how clinicians need to be sensitive to the differences between two parts of the same culture. The fact that the clinician's own ethnicity is not addressed does not take away from its impact. Rather, it is the authors' acknowledgement that all mental health professionals, regardless of ethnicity, must be aware of their own belief systems before treating individuals and families.

Case # 1: The Rodriquez Family

The Rodriquez family was initially referred because of their concern about their 15 year old son, John, who was apparently smoking marijuana with neighborhood teens. The mother, Rosa, (age 41) was born in Puerto Rico and came from a very traditional, rural, working class family which immigrated to New York in the late 1950's. The father, Juan, (age 43) was also Puerto Rican but from a more educated, middle class family. The couple, married for 15 years, frequently returns to Puerto Rico to visit relatives there. Juan recently lost his job and Rosa suspects his drinking to be the cause. After an initial family interview the clinician invited Juan to discuss the family's problems in an individual session.

T.   Juan, your wife says you drink too much, is that so?

J.   No, she just blames me because John smokes grass.

T.   I thought she was angry because you lost your job. Do you drink when you are angry at her?

J.   That's it! If I call her at 7:00 p.m. to say I'm on my way home, she starts yelling about the bad influence of my co-workers so I stay out for a few more drinks.

T.   It must be humiliating as a Latino man when Rosa thinks you are not a positive role model for your son, especially after losing your job.

J.   You don't know what I go through. My son agrees that she humiliates me in front of him. *She* needs therapy, not us.

T.   Your position as a proud father must be respected, of course. But I am concerned about your drinking. Let me tell you why. In the Latino/a culture, a man can lose some control but he must always be able to "drink like a man" (i.e., heavy consumption of hard liquor with minimal functional impairment). To be a good role model in the family is difficult if you are drinking.

J.   When I drink I don't lose control. My father always drank and controlled his liquor. He was very proud of that.

T.   I can understand you are proud. But some people may question your dignity and respect because of this drinking.

J.   I don't want people to judge me for my drinking. My conduct is always appropriate.

T.   True, but when your own family sees drinking as a problem, it is hard to feel good about yourself. Your dignity and respect are hurting.

J.   I feel bad about myself because I lost my job. People think I got fired because of my drinking. They drink even more than I do. It's not fair! *Me siento avergonzado* (I feel ashamed).

T. I'm going to ask you not to drink for a few days. Alcohol tranquilizes and depresses the mind. Can you do this?

J. *Claro que si* (of course).

T. Good Juan, this will give us a chance to understand how the family handles stress, especially your son's grass smoking and your job loss. I would like permission to meet with the family, with Rosa and then John. From now on, you and I will deal with the drinking issue separately from your son's problem. How is that?

J. I'll tell Rosa not to mention the drinking in front of John.

T. Fine, I look forward to our sessions together.

Discussion

The decision to see the father alone was designed to establish trust and to address the powerlessness of his position. The latin culture's support of heavy drinking which is associated with the *machismo* concept of *un hombre completo* (a complete man) directly conflicts with the values of dignity and respect. Placing this conflict within the culture freed the client of his guilt about drinking. Since social image and social role express human individuality, this clinical intervention maintained the client's identity intact. The clinician demonstrated a respect for Juan's sense of social role loss by reframing the drinking as a culturally-prescribed method of handling stress, not as the root of the family's problems. Then the clinician relieved another element of guilt by removing the client's responsibility for the "loss of control" aspect of drinking, given that the addiction may have been an unpredicted effect of the culture's prescription. The clinician directed the client not to drink in order to engage him in an exploration of the emotional/physical and the psychological/social effects of alcohol. In order to enter this dysfunctional system from a universal, non-threatening stance, the clinician framed the client's feelings in his own cultural terms and values.

CONCLUSION

Respect, dignity and trust are the icons of Latino/a culture. Clinicians who treat immigrants and their families, especially those who abuse alcohol or drugs, must be exquisitely sensitive to their place in the daily lives of their patients. This article provides a brief introduction to a new culture-sensitive model of integrating these values into assessments and intervention.

NOTE

1. The term *Latino* will be used to refer to peoples from Central and South America and the Caribbean/Atlantic region who have immigrated to English speaking North America. While recognizing the differences among each *Latino* group, the authors have chosen to focus on the Puerto Rican community as it reflects a majority of the national, cultural values, as well as some of the primary issues involved in the Latino immigrational experience.

BIBLIOGRAPHY

Aguirre-Molina, M. (1990). *Reaching women about alcohol and other drugs: Issues for Latinas – Puerto Rican women*. Metuchen, New Jersey: Scarecrow Press.

Comas-Dias, R. (1981). Puerto Rican espiritismo and psychotherapy: Ethnicity and treatment. *American Journal of Orthopsychiatry, 5*, (October), 1-4.

Comas-Dias, L. and Griffith, E. (1988). *Clinical guidelines in cross-cultural mental health*. New York: John Wiley and Sons, Inc.

De La Cancela (1986). A Critical analysis of Puerto Rican machismo: Implications for clinical practice. *Psychotherapy, 23*, (Summer).

Fernandez-Pol, B., Bluestone, H., Morales, G., and Mizrachi, M. (1985). Cultural Influences and Alcoholism: A Study of Puerto Ricans, *Alcoholism: Clinical and Experimental. 9*(5), 443-446.

Garcia-Preto, N. (1982). Puerto Rican families. In M. McGoldrick, J.K. Pearch, & J. Giordano (Eds.), *Ethnicity and Family Therapy*. New York: Guilford Press. (p. 166).

Ghali-Badillo, S., "Culture Sensitivity and the Puerto Rican Client," *Social Casework*. October 1977:459-463.

Gomez, A., "Ethnicity and Transculturality: Its Relevancy in Training Personnel to Work with Clients with Dependency Disorder." In Schecter, A. J. (ed.) *Drug Dependency and Alcoholism*. Vol. 2: Social and Behavioral Issues. New York, NY: Plenum Press.

Inclan, J. and Herron, G., "Puerto Rican Adolescents," *Children of Color*, Gibbs, J.T. and Huang, L.N. (eds.), Chapter 8, Jossey-Bass, 1989.

_____ "Variations in Value Orientation in Mental Health Work with Puerto Ricans," *Psychotherapy*, 22, Summer 1985.

_____ "Family Organization, Acculturation and Psychological Symptomatology in Second Generation Puerto Rican Women of Three Socio-Economic Class Groups," *Dissertation Abstract International*, *40*(4), 1980.

Melus, A., "Culture and Language in the Treatment of Alcoholism: The Hispanic Perspective," *Alcohol Health and Research World*, 1980, *3*:19-20.

Mizio, E., "The Impact of Macro Systems on Puerto Rican Families," in Powell, Gloria et al., eds., *The Psychosocial Development of Minority Group Children*. New York: Brunner/Mazel, 1983:216-236.

Mizio, E., "Impact of External Social Casework Systems on the Puerto Rican Family," *Social Casework*. February 1974.

Ramos-Rivera, Alba Nydia, *"Hacia Una Psychoterpia para el Puertorriqueno,"* Centro para Estudio y Desarrollo de la Personalidad Puertorriquena (Le Depp), 1984.

Rodriguez, C., *Puerto Ricans Born in the U.S.A.*, Unwin Hyman, Inc., Winchester, Mass. 1989.

Scharf, W.A., *Co-dependence*, New York: Harper and Row, 1986.

Zambrana, R., (ed.) *Work, Family and Health: Latina Women in Transition*, Monograph No. 7, Fordham University Hispanic Research Center, Bronx, NY 1982.

Treating Chemically Dependent Black Clients and Their Families

Stacia Murphy

SUMMARY. The provision of treatment to Blacks who have chemically dependent problems is both difficult and complex. A discussion of this treatment will target Black chemically dependent clients who have been involved in the criminal justice system and the approaches used to provide treatment to them and their family members.

SOME FACTS

Alcoholism ranks almost certainly as the number one mental health problem if not the most significant of all health problems in Black communities. It is tied to unemployment, crime, child abuse, broken families, and a host of other social problems (Bourne, 1973). King contends that alcoholism is the number one health problem in the Black community (1982).

Alcohol abuse is a primary health problem contributing to reduced longevity in the Black community. High incidence of acute and chronic alcohol related diseases among Blacks, such as alcoholic fatty liver, hepatitis, and cirrhosis of the liver; heart disease and cancer of the mouth, larynx, tongue, esophagus, and lung; and unintentional injures and homicide point to its endemic nature (Ronan, 1987).

An estimated fifty percent of federal prison system inmates, and nearly eighty percent of state prison inmates, have had experience

Stacia Murphy is Executive Director, Alcoholism Council/Fellowship Center, New York City, NY. Ms. Murphy lectures extensively and is adjunct faculty at the New School for Social Research. Correspondence may be sent to 49 E. 21st St., New York, NY 10010.

157

with drug use or addiction (Office of National Drug Control Policy, 1990). It has been documented that African Americans make up over half of the prison population nationally.

The previous citations adequately state the case that alcohol and other drug abuse has an overwhelmingly devastating and destructive effect on the Black community. What these authors began documenting as a serious problem over ten years ago continues. It perhaps suggests that members of the Black community have not made much progress in finding a solution. These data point to several issues that need to be addressed if we are to begin to stem the increase in the problem: a lack of basic knowledge and history regarding chemical dependency in the Black community; a distrust of the service delivery system which limits access to treatment facilities; a tendency among Blacks to let abuse problems progress to a chronic stage before seeking help; a lack of acceptance of alcohol/drug abuse as a health care issue which significantly impacts the quality of life in the Black community; and a sense of powerlessness that anything can be done.

IN RESPONSE

Many Black practitioners in the field of addiction have written that the treatment process for Blacks must be culturally sensitive and environmental resources and supports made to be a part of treatment. That may be an oversimplification.

When we speak of treatment, we must consider that Blacks are less likely to seek treatment for problem drinking than any other group. Treatment methodologies for the 1990's and the future must have a multimodal approach for Black alcoholics, and family involvement is paramount in the treatment of the Black alcoholic/addict (Brown and Tooley, 1984).

Beginning the treatment process for the chemically dependent client who is either on probation or parole can be an easy *and* difficult process. Easy, because these men and women are mandated to treatment. Their use and abuse of mood altering chemicals causes them to engage in criminal activity, and they feel that they don't have a choice. Difficult, because of strong denial about their alcohol and other drug use, and the feeling that they are again doing something against their will. Their drinking and drug taking is for reasons related to things outside of themselves. This is also a common feeling among family members, with the result that both depersonalize the problem and blame others and each other.

Thus, in the initial contact, referring here to outpatient treatment, it is very important that the client feel 'safe,' that is, unjudged and unimpinged upon. The atmosphere in the organizational environment is critical. It must treat the client with dignity and respect, articulate boundaries and limits, have clearly defined goals and expectations, engage the client in a process of personal investment in recovery, and, most of all, assist in the development of skills necessary in order for the client to maintain abstinence and support the struggle that each individual has in trying to achieve the goal of abstinence and self acceptance. The staff must be well trained, have a psychologically "affective" understanding of addiction, be knowledgeable about treatment, have their own healthy psyche, and believe in the ability of the client to change. They must understand the shame associated with the client's addiction problem as well as prison incarceration. That shame contributes to the negative behavior of the client and determines negative responses if he has not learned how to tolerate feelings of discomfort and dis-ease. And finally, that shame manifests itself primarily through anger of the client and family members.

The safe quality of the environment serves to embrace and nurture the client within a structure of discipline, warmth and openness that invites participation. This first contact, the intake and assessment, must communicate to the client acceptance. It must accomplish one goal: the client should feel better about the experience and return for his next appointment.

Information gathered in the first meeting establishes a guide for the counselor to pursue. Since the client has been mandated to treatment it is understood that he has some chemically dependent problem. The assessment should determine the progression of the illness and identify at-risk situations that can threaten the recovery process.

Since denial is a common defense mechanism of chemically dependent clients, the clinician must be prepared to obtain corroborating information. In this case information could be retrieved from the parole officer or, if the client received 'treatment' while incarcerated, from the counselor in the correctional facility that he left.

Miller, Crawford and Taylor (1979) have recommended interviewing the significant others as sources of validating information. The approach to that recommendation will be addressed later in this chapter. However, self-disclosure and admitting that the problem exists is often not the difficulty for this population. Acceptance is. They are motivated by a fear of returning to chemical use that will result in reincarceration. They exhibit a strong will and determination to stay drug free. What they lack is information about chemical dependency, coping skills, positive survival behaviors and a healthy sense of themselves. This is exacerbated by the double stigma of being alcoholics/addicts and Black ex-offenders. Thus they do not feel a part of the mainstream and tend to remain socially isolated from the healthier components of their environment. Getting this population to treatment is important. Getting them to stay depends on how they are engaged.

TREATMENT

There was a time not long ago when therapists were trained in a "one true light" tradition. A would-be professional chose to be trained in one of several rival schools of treatment and was thoroughly indoctrinated into that perspective. The subtleties of practice in that mode were expounded, and an impelling rationale for the superiority of this approach was learned by heart along with the faults and failures of all other approaches to treatment. Each student of therapy was taught that his or hers was the one correct way toward the lasting alleviation of human suffering (Miller & Hester, 1989).

As we learn more about addiction and its effects on diverse populations, we must become less rigid, and acknowledge the need for disciplined, less defensive and more experimental approaches. This supports the concern of treatment for Blacks and conflicts with the beliefs or myths that

1. Nothing works.
2. There is one particular approach which is superior to all others.
3. All treatment approaches work about equally well.

(Miller & Hester, 1989)

There exists a large body of treatment research now available which indicates that there are several different approaches significantly better than no intervention or alternative treatments useful to practitioners to learn if we are to provide effective treatment to the Black chemically dependent population and their families. No one approach stands out from all the rest, but neither are all treatments equally effective (or ineffective). The reason for hope and optimism in the alcoholism field is not the presence of a single outstandingly effective approach but rather an array of promising and effective alternatives, each of which may be most effective for different types of individuals. For most individuals, the chances are good for finding an acceptable and effective intervention among these choices (Miller & Hester, 1989).

This eclecticism supports and encourages the assertions made by other clinicians that treatment for the Black addict must be multimodal. Williams (1982) discussed the need for cultural specific approaches that involve understanding the clients frame of reference and incorporating it into therapeutic strategies to maximize their effectiveness. Since Blacks are not a homogenous group and have both class and cultural differences, it has been suggested by Morgan (1986) that matching the ethnicity of the counselor and the addict as well as developing cultural sensitive treatment programs are not enough to help the minority addict recover. Indeed, a critical first step in recovery is to address the drug problem. If it causes the problem it is the problem.

Three factors important to sobriety are (1) recognition and acceptance of the problem, (2) awareness of the reason for using drugs and, (3) a self interest to refrain from drug taking and learning how to stay stopped.

In this context we integrate several models as an effective approach to this group. The American disease model establishes the rationale for abstinence. This is important for the Black chemically dependent person because of the tendency toward the use of illicit drugs, the lack of acceptance that alcohol is a drug, and this use in the Black community because it is legal and a vehicle to forget troubles. The education model supports the assumption that alcohol and other drug problems evolve from a knowledge deficit, and a lack of accurate information (Miller & Hester, 1989). This population surely exhibits that deficit. The use of this model allows for engagement of the client in the therapeutic activities that begin to change the way he/she thinks as well, influencing a change in attitudes. The social learning model utilizes an approach that emphasizes the need for the development of healthy coping skills and views 'modeling' as a cause of the clients developing addiction problems. This conversely can be an influence in avoiding relapse.

Interventions from a social learning perspective focus on altering the person's relationship to his or her environment. Changes must be made in the person's circle of friends, to avoid exposure to negative models and further reinforcement for problematic drinking. New skills must be taught so that the person need not rely upon a drug for coping purposes. Cognitive restructuring must be used in an attempt to alter positive expectancies derived from alcohol and drug use. Preventive interventions within this model are concerned with conditions of the social environment that foster positive expectations for alcohol use, provide heavy-drinking role models, or encourage the use of alcohol and other drugs to cope with problems (Hester & Miller, 1989).

The sociocultural model addresses the issue of societal attitudes and as this chapter has suggested the attitudes about alcohol and drug use in the Black community, which is the availability and the level of societal stress and alienation that characterize being Black in America.

Our experience in working with the Black chemically dependent addict is that which works for one may not work for another. However, in utilizing approaches that allow flexibility and address the most immediate need of the client are what induce the client to stay and begin to change.

Family involvement in treatment is an absolute necessity if treatment is to have a chance of working. Family members for this group must be engaged in a similar process as the client. However, their reasons for coming or being invited to come need to be described because they determine how involved family members are then willing to become. Interestingly most come voluntarily but for different reasons, such as,

1. to support the efforts of the client in staying drug free and out of prison
2. to force the client to come to treatment because they have not been attending regularly
3. to report the resumption of drug use by the client
4. to work through difficulties that are arising because of the clients involvement in treatment and change
5. to address their own problems of addiction (usually initiated by the client)
6. to talk through confusion regarding a client still in prison who will be coming for treatment after release.

Each of these scenarios is often perceived by the client and/or the significant other as a 'one shot deal.' Most have not thought about or are prepared to start participation in treatment. They see it as outside of them, and this reinforces their denial.

Though there is an identified reason, an attempt is made to shift the focus away from the client to the significant other. However, their reasons are acknowledged and addressed as a way of establishing a rapport that allows the accomplishment of specific goals, such as

1. to develop an alliance
2. to educate and sensitize family members about addiction
3. to describe the process of treatment that the client is engaged in
4. to identify problems that may be threatening to the recovery of the client
5. to encourage and strengthen a natural and valuable support system
6. to address their issues that exist because of their relationship to the client

7. to provide a safe environment that encourages dialogue and problem solving
8. to reinforce in a positive way client treatment.

Over time, with the involvement of family members and clients talking separately and together, much of the stress that each experiences is identified and an attempt is made to help them understand that stress and learn how to manage it in a healthy way. The feelings of anger and lack of positive relating one to the other is usually the recurring theme in the treatment encounter.

Family relations can be stressful under any circumstances. For the Black client and the family that stress is usually exacerbated by other forces most of which are beyond their control. The focus of treatment must be directed toward helping them change themselves, and can be viewed as a process of empowerment so that they are more in control of their lives.

CONCLUSION

Treatment for the Black chemically dependent clients and their families is important and necessary given the destructiveness of its use in the Black community. Yes, it must be culturally sensitive and cater to the special needs that this group presents. However, people who are addicted must stop using drugs first or be motivated to stop if they are to be successful and healthy. Families must understand their roles and create environments to support both their change as well as their loved ones.

REFERENCES

Bourne, P. (1973). Alcoholism in the Urban Black Population. *Alcoholism: Progress in Research and Treatment* (work in progress).

Brown, F. & Tooley, J. (1990). Alcoholism in the Black Community. *Alcoholism and Substance Abuse in Special Populations*, 124-125.

Executive Office of the President, Office of National Drug Control Policy. (1990). *National Drug Control Strategy*, 17.

King, L.M. (1982). Alcoholism: Studies regarding black Americans 1977-1980. *Alcohol and Health Monograph No. 4, Special Population Issues*, 385-407.

Miller, W.R., Crawford, V.V., & Taylor, C. A. (1979). Significant others as corroborative sources for problem drinkers. *Addictive Behaviors, 4*, 67-70.

Miller, W.R. & Hester, R. V. (1989). Treating alcohol problems: Toward an informed eclecticism. *Handbook of Alcoholism Treatment Approaches*, 3-8.

Rogan, A. (1986). Recovery from alcoholism: Issues for black and Native American alcoholics. *Alcohol and Health Research World, II* (1), 42-44.

Ronan, L. (1987). Alcohol-related risk among black Americans. *Alcohol and Health Research World, 2-6*, 36-39.

Williams, M., (1982). Blacks and alcoholism: Issues in the 1980's. *Alcohol and Health Research World, 6* (4), 31-40.

Assessment and Treatment
of the Mentally Ill Chemical Abuser
and the Family

Phyllis G. Reilly, MA, CAC

SUMMARY. The Mentally Ill Chemical Abuser is a challenge to both mental health and chemical dependency providers and requires an integrated collaborative approach. Guidelines for comprehensive assessment are presented. Treatment issues such as pharmacological interventions and abstinence are raised. Characteristics of chemically dependent and mentally ill chemical abuser families are compared. Family therapy and family management approaches which focus on education about the illness and skill building behaviors are advanced. An integrated, collaborative approach is recommended.

This article addresses pertinent issues surrounding a growing and complex treatment population, mentally ill chemical abusers (MICA). Because of their dual, coexisting problems of both chemical dependence and a major psychiatric disorder, MICA clients present a unique challenge in service delivery. Traditionally eschewed by both addiction and mental health professionals, this population has been misdiagnosed, mistreated, and misdirected. To date, although there is much concern and interest, there has been no nationally recognized "state of the art" of MICA service delivery (Reilly & Woods, 1989).

Practitioners in both chemical dependency and mental health dis-

Phyllis G. Reilly is Director of Addiction Recovery Services, UMDNJ-CMHC at Piscataway, NJ. She co-directs a nationally recognized clinical model and psychosocial MICA program. Correspondence may be sent to UMDNJ-CMHC at Piscataway, Addiction Recovery Services, 667 Hoes Lane, Piscataway, NJ 08854.

ciplines are encouraged to utilize an integrated, collaborative approach. Most important are comprehensive assessments which yield accurate differential diagnoses and pave the way for appropriate treatment. Unfortunately, family management approaches are minimally included as part of the MICA treatment process. Family therapy techniques and less threatening family education methods are critical and have been successful in ensuring the stability of the MICA relative and the functional reorganization of the family.

PREVALENCE OF THE PROBLEM

Although definitive prevalence data is still to be compiled, recent research and needs assessment statistics reveal that a majority of chemical abusers suffer from some sort of additional psychopathology. In fact, Helzer and Pryzbeck's report on the findings of the Epidemiological Catchment Area Study (1988) confirmed that 13 percent of 20,000 adult subjects had a diagnosis of chronic alcohol abuse and dependence, and, of those, nearly half had an additional diagnosis. The study indicated a significant over representation of concurrent psychopathology with an alcohol diagnosis. Hesselbrock, Meyer, and Keener (1984) found that 75% of men and 80% of women in a client sample at three inpatient alcoholism treatment centers were verified MICA clients. Weissman, Myers, and Harding (1980) found a 70% MICA prevalence rate in a community mental health center sample with a diagnosis of alcohol abuse. Tarter, McBride, Buonopane, and Schneider (1977) found a 67% MICA prevalence rate in Veterans Administration male alcoholics, and Robbins (1975) found a 70% MICA prevalence rate among alcoholics who were seen in the emergency room of a general hospital. Talbott (1987) theorized that among young chronic, mentally ill clients (18 to 40 years old) the incidence of substance abuse might be as high as 50 percent. The work of Pepper and Ryglewicz (1984) substantiated this theory and focused on use patterns of the most common but often undetected substances—alcohol and marijuana. Client service data collected by the New Jersey Division of Mental Health and Hospitals (1987) attested to the magnitude of the problem: 30,000 to 40,000 clients statewide were MICA; of these,

30 to 50% of all hospital and more than a third of all community mental health agency admissions were MICA.

A substantial body of research is devoted to determining which disorders came first and which are more prevalent. Hesselbrock et al. have shown that for MICA women the onset of most psychopathologies preceded the abuse of alcohol, while for men the reverse was true, with the exception of men suffering from antisocial personality and panic disorders. The psychiatric disorders most commonly associated with chemical abuse and dependency have been enumerated by several authors. Daley, Moss and Campbell (1987) and Bernadt and Murray (1986) in their separate studies of alcoholics listed a number of concurrent disorders in a rough epidemiological order: personality disorders (antisocial and borderline), affective disorders (major depression, dysthymic, and bipolar disorders), anxiety disorders (phobic and anxiety states), the various types of schizophrenia, and the organic brain syndromes (amnesia and dementia). Hesselbrock et al. found that the most prevalent co-occurring psychopathologies for men were antisocial personality, then major depression; for women, depression, then phobia. Most of these studies used the Diagnostic Interview Schedule and the DSM-IIIR criteria to formulate diagnoses (American Psychiatric Association, 1987).

DEFINITION OF THE MICA

Definitions of the mentally ill chemical abuser present a fragmented view of the population. Daley utilized the term Dual Diagnosis to refer to the concurrent diagnosis of alcoholism as well as a psychiatric diagnosis. McClellan (1979) and Tsuang (1982), on the other hand, focused on drug abusers with psychosis (DAP). Tsuang, in particular, distinguished between several distinct psychiatric subgroups, especially those with schizophrenia. Pepper (1984) and Talbott (1987) focused on the young adult with chronic mental illness (primarily schizophrenia) and diagnosed substance abuse problems by history or use of alcohol and other drugs. Several terms throughout the nation are used to define this population that suffers from concurrent psychiatric illness and substance use disorders: PICA (Psychiatric Impaired Chemical Abuser), MISA

(Mentally Ill Substance Abuser), SAMI (Substance Abusing Mentally Ill) and Double Trouble. These acronyms are generally preferred to the term dual diagnosis which has been used in the past to refer to clients who abuse both alcohol and drugs. The New Jersey Division of Mental Health and Hospitals MICA Committee definition (1987) has been accepted and utilized statewide and also has been adopted by other states as their model operational definition. This definition (espoused by the author) does not advocate a particular treatment philosophy nor methodology but, rather, describes individuals:

> Who have had or are presently demonstrating significant symptoms of severe psychopathology of a chronic or relapsing course. Such individuals must meet the diagnostic criteria for both major psychiatric disorders and for substance dependence; . . . and must show significant functional impairment in . . . self-care, socialization, and employment.

The definition includes chronic relapsers and excludes persons under the age of 18, the more higher functioning MICA clients or those who abuse alcohol and other drugs without any pathological and chronic effects. The definition is now in the process of revision to include the seriously emotionally ill chemical abusing adolescent (SEICA) as well as higher functioning MICA clients.

Caragonne (1987) found that the fragmentation of MICA definition apparent in both the fields of psychopathology and substance abuse resulted in restricting providers to one-dimensional definitions and one-dimensional causation models. She indicated that depending upon one's theoretical framework (chemical dependency or psychopathology), the most familiar set of factors in the definition and in the model would be emphasized to the exclusion of others. She predicated that a broader definition which examined the scope of the problem and the continuum of the diagnosis would be beneficial to both providers and to clients and serve to enhance assessment and treatment planning as well as provision of other services.

ASSESSMENT GUIDELINES

Assessments present a thorny problem for addiction and mental health professionals. Often, active addiction masks a preexisting undiagnosed psychiatric illness or a preexisting diagnosed psychiatric illness will mask active addiction. Many treatment professionals become lost in trying to diagnose which came first and wander about in a diagnostic "chicken or egg" maze. What is key is that addiction and mental health providers must identify the concomitant illnesses which then must be appropriately treated. A comprehensive assessment of the MICA should include several significant components which bridge both disciplines: a thorough psychiatric history; a thorough substance abuse history; a medical history including current physical problems; a physical exam and laboratory tests including drug and alcohol screens; family, social and self-help support histories; educational history, vocational history, criminal justice involvement; religious history and spiritual functioning; and interpersonal functioning, family support, self-help and recreational activities. Especially critical are the perceptions and observations of the interviewer. Also required is information from other sources than the client and family such as gatekeeper agencies, other treatment facilities, records reviews, and collateral interviews. There should be a thorough review of utilization of prescription medications, over-the-counter drugs, an exploration of housing needs and at risk behaviors (especially involving the use of intravenous drugs), and possible testing for HIV infection. Once the assessment data is compiled, an initial diagnosis should be formulated (under DSMIII-R, Axis I) listing both a substance use disorder as well as a psychiatric disorder. As the client stabilizes from either disorder, the diagnoses may change. Therefore, the author underscores that assessment be viewed as an ongoing process and that a client must be reevaluated during each phase of treatment. At some point, the psychiatric illness will be dominant and one form of treatment will be appropriate and, at other times, the substance use disorder will be active and another form of treatment will be essential. As practitioners become more sophisticated in assessment techniques through the use of structured client and family interviews, observation, laboratory testing, clinical records reviews, and multi-disciplinary team reviews, the differential diagnoses will be accurate and facilitate treatment planning for the dual diagnosed client and family.

TREATMENT ISSUES

The use of medication, the demand for abstinence, the use of self-help groups, and the practice of drug monitoring are issues which have polarized addiction and mental health professionals. Appropriate psychotropic medication is required to stabilize psychiatric illness while abstinence is fundamental to recovery from addiction. However, because so many addicted clients have been inappropriately medicated by mental health practitioners, some untrained addiction professionals have admonished clients to abstain from necessary medications. Clients have suffered as a result of these professional misdirections. Some New Jersey MICA programs celebrate 30 days of client abstinence rather than the traditional AA 90 days. Thirty days for a MICA is a major achievement as recovery is more complicated and there are more relapses than with other clients. Abstinence, then, must be viewed within the continuum of recovery from concomitant illnesses. An emergent treatment issue involves the formation and training of a multi-disciplinary team to treat the MICA. The New Jersey MICA Committee's recommendations for the composition of the team range from a board eligible or certified psychiatrist, nurse, to mental health, psychosocial and addiction counselors. Ongoing training and collaboration among the disciplines is essential. Otherwise, discipline and treatment culture biases are translated into turf battles and professional controversies which cloud client needs and hamper appropriate treatment. Another issue which causes concern is the utilization of strong ongoing community support networks such as AA, NA, and Al-Anon. While these twelve-step programs have proven to be extremely effective for many years in helping addicts to maintain abstinence and to adjust to chemical free living, many MICA have felt stigmatized and criticized at these self-help group meetings. In response to MICA self-help group needs, a special AA and NA meeting for the MICA client (originally called "Double Trouble") was initiated in New Jersey in 1981. There are now similar meetings in many communities throughout the United States which address significant aspects of the dual diagnosis.

Another critical treatment issue concerns drug monitoring. Addiction professionals view drug monitoring as a valuable component of treatment while mental health professionals tend to view drug testing as a necessary evil which interferes with the client counselor trust relationship. In practice, drug monitoring serves to help MICA clients meet abstinence goals and limits their denial of chemical use.

CHARACTERISTICS OF CHEMICALLY DEPENDENT FAMILIES

While research on the MICA client's family system is nonexistent, there are several anecdotal case studies available in regional and statewide MICA newsletters. On the other hand, the alcoholic or drug dependent family system has been extensively described and studied (Wegscheider, 1981; Kaufman, 1985; Steinglass, 1985; Black, 1982; and Black, Bucky & Wilder-Padilla, 1986). Parallels can certainly be drawn between the MICA client's family structure and the alcoholic or drug dependent client's family structure. Indeed, the author has seen more severe psychosocial and physical dysfunctions with the MICA client's family system than the addicted client's. For example, Stanton and Todd (1982) found several areas of dysfunction in the family system of drug abusers: high frequency of multigenerational chemical dependency; primitive and direct expression of conflict with explicit alliances; mothers with symbiotic child-rearing practices extending into the child's later life, and incidence of premature, unexpected or untimely deaths.

Kaufman and Pattison (1981) characterized dysfunctional alcoholic or drug abusing families as follows: these families were often neurotic and enmeshed, showed evidence of rigidity, disorganization, unclear communication and boundaries, isolation, and role conflict and reversal.

Steinglass (1985) approached the problem of alcoholism in families with theoretical models specifying two core concepts of the alcoholic family system: The first core construct — morphostasis —

predicted that all families tended to establish and then behave in balanced and stable ways resisting changes from this predetermined level of stability. The second core construct (morphogenesis) predicted that families invariably moved toward greater organizational complexity over time. In his view, alcoholic families became dysfunctional because they invested almost all psychic and physical energy in morphostatic states to the exclusion of morphogenic states.

FAMILY THERAPY
AND FAMILY MANAGEMENT APPROACHES

While mental health and addiction practitioners have embraced family therapy and family management techniques in working with either mentally ill or addicted family members, there has been limited application of these approaches with the MICA family. However, the author's experience with several hundred MICA families attests to the efficacy of family therapy and family management techniques with this population. Mental health practitioners seem more inclined to employ family therapy techniques at all phases of treatment with the MICA whereas chemical dependency practitioners have tended to use family management techniques in the recovery phase and focus more on the needs of the addict by decreasing the denial of the family, encouraging the family to accept the addiction as well as the mental illness, and coaching the family to create a climate conducive to recovery. Further, both strategic and structural family therapy approaches have been beneficial in working with the MICA. For example, the indirect techniques of strategic therapists (Haley, 1976) which use prescriptions and paradoxical instruction and work toward second order change have been useful in treating MICA families in crisis. The structural techniques which emphasize restoring homeostasis in the family by dealing with alliances, triangles, and boundaries have been especially suited to the recovery phase and later stages of treatment. Family support groups for the MICA are virtually nonexistent. However, families with psychiatrically disabled adolescents and adults have formed consumer advocacy and support groups (such as the National Alliance for the Mentally Ill and the New Jersey Concerned Citizens for Chronic Psychiatric Adults). There is an urgent need for Al-Anon groups and similar support groups specifically for MICA families. It is the author's bias that families with MICA members have greater denial, stigma, feelings of hopelessness and frustration and distrust of the professional system than families with a relative with a single diagnosis. By personal observation these families behave in predictable patterns when they are confronted with a relative with a dual diagnosis. At first they deny the problem, then they try to solve the problem overnight. They are grandiose about their ability to help their relative but they often fail to follow through consistently. Often, their frustration and distrust of the health care system pushes them to pursue courses of action which impede recovery. Because they feel powerless over one illness they feel doubly powerless over two illnesses. Understandably, they need reassurance and they are especially sensitive to criticism and to chemical dependency approaches (e.g., the enabler concept) which seem to blame them for the illnesses. For these reasons, family support and multifamily groups should be incorporated into MICA programs. For those clients who do not have an intact or supportive family, non traditional family groups have been created. These peer families are prevalent in psychosocial rehabilitation environments or supervised housing situations. Peer family support has helped MICA clients to maintain sobriety and mental wellness. Indeed, family groups have helped to stabilize those families in crisis, those families facing reentry of their relative after a hospitalization, and those with ongoing recovery issues.

One of the most important components of MICA family management is the institution of family education and skill development programs. Families require a firm foundation and understanding of the dynamics of psychiatric illnesses as well as chemical dependency and, in addition, they require a repertoire of skills in order to cope effectively with a MICA relative. Family education, less threatening than family therapy, has helped MICA families to reduce negative symptoms of both illnesses and to ease the burden that they carry with regard to having relatives with both illnesses.

Family education is especially helpful because families learn about the illness in a blame free environment and feel more receptive to trying new approaches with their relatives (Hatfield, 1989). Family management is also helpful in that families are coached to communicate more effectively with their MICA relative, to have more realistic expectations of their relative's recovery and to become less critical and demanding of the relative in view of the dual diagnosis. Families are also instructed in the danger signs of relapse. Finally, families are trained to call family meetings and meetings with the practitioners to discuss family rules and roles and appropriate behavior for the MICA relative.

CONCLUSION

Today, the mentally ill chemical abuser, no matter how broad or narrowly defined, is a common and challenging occurrence in both mental health and chemical dependency treatment. The MICA client requires a collaborative, integrated approach with appropriate assessment and treatment to overcome the concurrent illnesses. Further, family therapy and family management approaches have been demonstrated to be effective in maintaining the gains made by MICA family relatives, in helping the family to face denial, in restoring balance, and in decreasing psychotic episodes and chemical dependency relapses. Strategic and structural family therapy techniques as well as chemical dependency treatment standbys such as family education and skill building behavior techniques have proven successful for MICA families. A combination of these family focused approaches will help to facilitate family support and recovery, ensure ongoing treatment gains, and restore the MICA client to independent functioning within the family and the community.

REFERENCES

American Psychiatric Association. (1987). *Diagnostic and statistical manual of mental disorders* (3rd rev. ed.). Washington, D.C.: Author.

Bernadt, M.W., & Murray, R.M. (1986). Psychiatric disorder, drinking and alcoholism: What are the links? *British Journal of Psychiatry, 148*, 393-400.

Black, C. (1982). *It will never happen to me: Children of alcoholics as youngsters, adolescents, adults.* Colorado: MAC.

Black, C., Bucky, S.F., & Wilder-Padilla, S. (1986). The Interpersonal and emotional consequences of being an adult child of an alcoholic. *The International Journal of Addiction, 21*, 213-231.

Caragonne, P. (1987). Mental illness and substance abuse: The dually diagnosed client. *Monograph of the National Council of Community Mental Centers. 2.* (Series: Clinical).

Daley, D.C., Moss, H., & Campbell, F. (1987). *Dual disorders: Counseling clients with chemical dependency and mental illness.* Minneapolis, MN: Hazelden.

Haley, J. (1976) *Problem Solving Therapy.* San Francisco, CA: Jossey-Bass.

Hatfield, A.B. (1989). *Family education in mental illness.* New York: Guilford Press.

Helzer, J. & Pryzbeck, T.R. (1988). The co-occurrence of alcoholism with other psychiatric disorders in the general population and its impact on treatment. *Journal of Studies on Alcohol, 49*, 219-224.

Hesselbrock, M.N., Meyer, R.E., & Keener J.J. (1985). Psychopathology in hospitalized alcoholics. *Archives of General Psychiatry, 42*, 1050-1055.

Kaufman, E. (1985). Family systems and family therapy of substance abuse: An overview of two decades of research and clinical experience. *The International Journal of the Addictions, 20*, 897-916.

Kaufman, E. & Pattison, E.M. (1981). Differential methods of family therapy in the treatment of alcoholism. *Journal of Studies on Alcohol, 42*, 951-971. 1979.

McLellan, A.T., Woody, G., & O'Brien, C. (1979). Development of psychiatric illness in drug abusers. *New England Journal of Medicine, 301*, 1310.

New Jersey Division of Mental Health and Hospitals. (1987). *Guidelines for continuum of care in MICA services.* Trenton, NJ: Author.

Pepper, B. & Rygelowicz, H. (1984). The young adult chronic patient and substance abuse. *Tie-Lines.*

Reilly, P. & Woods, J. (1989, October). *Special needs and problems of the mentally ill chemical abuser.* Paper presented at the meeting of the American Public Health Association, Chicago, IL.

Robbins, L.N. (1975). *Evaluation of the alcoholic: Implications for research, theory, and treatment* (Research Monograph No. 5). Washington, D.C.: National Institute of Alcoholism and Alcohol Abuse.

Stanton, M.D. & Todd, T.C. (1982). *The family therapy of drug abuse and addiction.* New York: Guilford Press.

Steinglass, P. (1985). Family systems approaches to alcoholism. *Journal of Substance Abuse Treatment, 2*, 161-167.

Talbott, J.A., Ridgely, M.S., Osher, F.C. & Goldman, H.H. (1987) *Executive summary: Chronic mentally ill young adults with substance abuse problems.* Baltimore: University of Maryland, School of Medicine.

Tarter, R.E., McBride, H., Buonpane, N. & Schneider, D. (1987). Differentiation of alcoholics: Childhood history of minimal brain functions, family history, and drinking pattern. *Archives of General Psychiatry, 34*, 761-768.

Tsuang, M.T., Simpson, J.C. & Kronfal, Z. (1982). Subtypes of Drug Abuse with Psychosis: Demographic characteristics, clinical features and family history. *Archives of General Psychiatry, 39*, 141-147.

Wegscheider, S. (1981). *Another chance: Hope and health for the alcoholic family.* Palo Alto, CA: Science and Behavior Books.

Weissman, M.M., Meyers, J.K. & Harding, P.S. (1980). Prevalence and psychiatric heterogeneity of alcoholism in a US urban community. *Journal of Studies on Alcohol, 41*, 672-681.

Index

structural family therapy role,
48-49
triangulation, 48,50
Todd, Thomas, 8
Transference, 42,46,52,53-54
Trauma fix, 83-84
Triangulation, 8,32,174
Bowen's family therapy model,
50,51,55
of therapist, 48,50
Trust
in chemically-dependent families,
65
as Latino cultural value, 139
Twelve-step programs. *See also*
Alcoholics Anonymous;
Narcotics Anonymous
family systems therapy and,
87-109
assessment, 99-100
Bowen's model, 98-99
differentiation, 93,95,106,107
differentiation versus
disengagement, 95
"dry systems", 97,98,103,104,
105
in early sobriety, 103-106
as "healthy family" metaphor,
95
"hitting bottom" concept, 98,
99,101,102
homeostasis, 100,104
individual counseling versus,
90-91
intervention as process,
102-103
in late sobriety, 106
reframing technique, 101
"wet systems", 97,98,100,
101,103,104,105
for mentally-ill chemical abusers,
172-173

Minnesota Model, 89
professional rehabilitation
programs and, 89-90
self-responsibility concept, 91-93
steps of, 91-93
as structural intervention, 33
Twin studies, of alcoholism, 10

Under the Influence (Elkin), 33

Values, Latino cultural, 138-153
alcoholism and, 141-153
Cultural Sensitive Assessment
Model, 147-153
case example, 151-153
clinical objectives, 147-148
guidelines, 148-151

Watzlawick, Paul, 33
Weakland, John, 33
Withdrawal, emotional, 20
Women, chemically-dependent,
111-119
addiction onset, 111-112
alcohol abuse-related health
problems, 112
case histories, 114-117
codependency, 115
divorce, 112
misdiagnosis, 113
social attitudes towards, 112,113
solitary drinking, 112
treatment
childcare arrangements and,
118
components, 117
family support for, 115
sex therapy, 118
treatment utilization, 113
Worthlessness, 78